LANSLEY 99

RIVERDALE PUBLIC LIBRARY DISTRICT

3 1163 00060 66

W9-BZX-165

DATE DUE

RIVERDALE
DATE DUE
06 30 03

5 05   DEMCO 128-8155

RIVERDALE PUBLIC LIBRARY
208 West 144th Street
Riverdale, Illinois 60627
Phone: (708) 841-3311

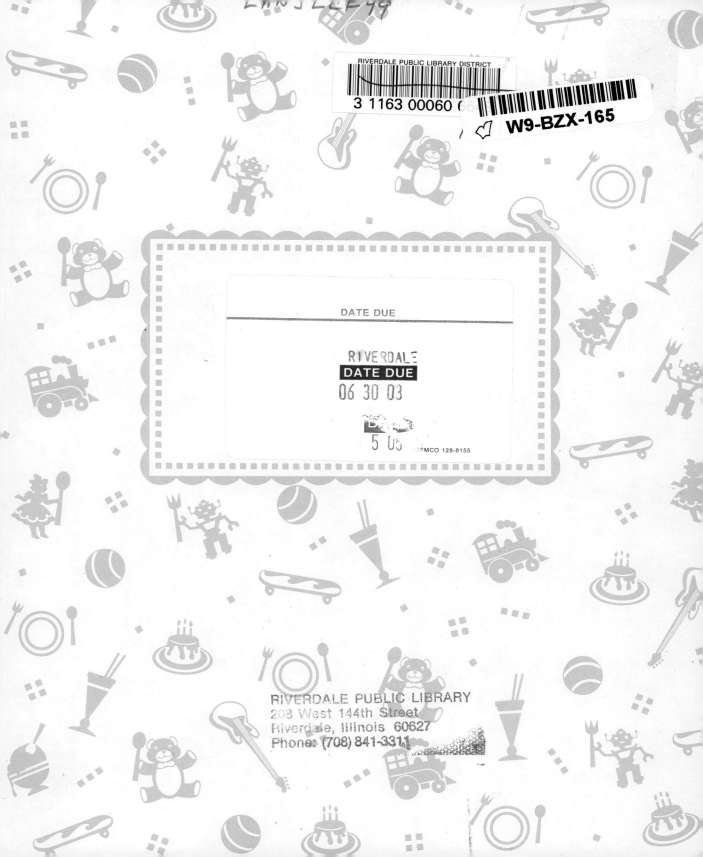

Jenifer Lang Cooks for Kids

Jenifer Lang Cooks for Kids

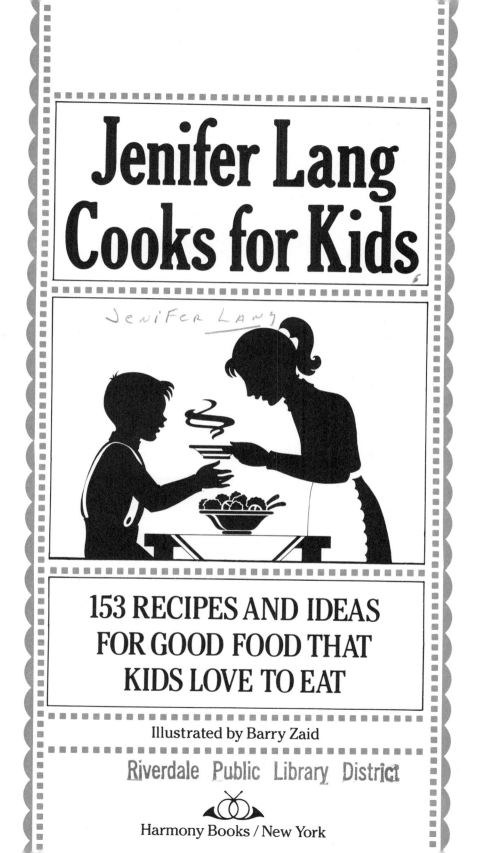

Jenifer Lang

153 RECIPES AND IDEAS FOR GOOD FOOD THAT KIDS LOVE TO EAT

Illustrated by Barry Zaid

Riverdale Public Library District

Harmony Books / New York

641.5
LAN

This book is dedicated to my mother, Kathlyn Free, who nourished my body, my heart and my spirit — not necessarily in that order.

Copyright © 1991 by Jenifer Lang
Illustrations copyright © 1991 by Barry Zaid

All rights reserved. No part of this book may be reproduced or
transmitted in any form or by any means, electronic or mechanical,
including photocopying, recording, or by any information storage and
retrieval system, without permission in writing from the publisher.

Published by Harmony Books, a division of Crown Publishers, Inc.,
201 East 50th Street, New York, New York 10022. Member of the Crown Publishing Group.

HARMONY and colophon are trademarks of Crown Publishers, Inc.
Manufactured in the United States of America

Library of Congress Cataloging-in-Publication Data

Lang, Jenifer Harvey.
[cooks for kids]
Jenifer Lang cooks for kids: 153 recipes and ideas for good foods that kids love to eat,
for infants through teenagers.—1st ed.
p.   cm.
Includes index.
1. Cookery. 2. Children—Nutrition. I. Title.
TX652.L246 1991
641.5′622—dc20   90-28378
CIP

ISBN 0-517-58417-4
10 9 8 7 6 5 4 3 2 1
First Edition

CONTENTS

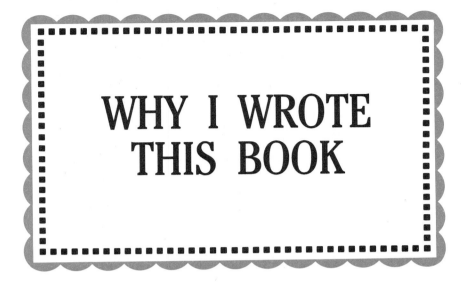

WHY I WROTE
THIS BOOK

Three years ago, when various friends began suggesting that I write a book of recipes for children, I dismissed the idea. I had gone through pregnancy and the birth of my son, Simon, reading dozens of helpful volumes on infants. I was sure there must be lots of equally good books on feeding kids.

As Simon grew older, I discovered this wasn't true. Although there *are* books on how to feed children, none of them speaks to me. Some taught the virtues of health food so effectively you feel that one trip to McDonald's and your child is doomed to a failed life. Others add to what Richard Saul Wurman calls "information anxiety"; they are jammed full of minutia such as vitamin K's role in blood clotting. Along about this time I realized I needed practical help feeding Simon, and since it didn't already exist, I decided to write a book of solutions to the most pressing problems of feeding a child.

Why I Wrote This Book

What problems? Well, I assume you have a child, so at the risk of highlighting the obvious:

1. I daresay that every child is picky (fussy, finicky—you supply your own word) at some time in his life, to one degree or another, even if it only means he won't eat tomatoes when you have a garden full of them. Other kids may have a food repertoire of four items, and *that's it.*

2. Make sure, as much as possible, that your child's diet is chock full of nutrients and whole foods. These days, that requires a sophisticated knowledge of food science.

3. One of the major food questions when kids are involved is, What am I going to make for dinner tonight? Those of us who take primary responsibility for the feeding of our children—and I guess I'm talking about mothers here more than fathers—know full well that the drudgery of cooking (or planning) three meals a day for a family often means resorting to standard dishes. The constraints of our schedules and of our imaginations prevent us from trying new things that will break our boring food routine and provide nutritional variety.

    To make this situation worse, if you have a small family (one or two kids) and decide to look up recipes in search of ideas, the yields are often discouraging, and you know you'll end up with a refrigerator full of leftovers when the meal is finished.

I wanted this book to re-create the experience of the play group Simon and I belonged to when he was about a year old. Six or seven children and their moms got together once a week, and invariably the conversation would turn to food. Someone would say, "You know what I made for Lucy last night? I poached a chicken breast, and then . . ." and the rest of us would try the same thing at home with our babies and husbands. We were looking for ideas and advice, and we often found them in these casual conversations.

Perhaps I was more troubled than the other mothers about feeding my child, since my professional life revolves around food and I know too much to be cavalier about eating. I must also confess that I have a lifetime of supercilious attitudes about food to overcome. (Having a child can be a humbling experience.)

While I was a student at the Culinary Institute of America, learning the intricacies of grand cuisine and fine wines, I spent a holiday with my mother. During one of our drive-time conversations, she let me go on and on about my study of gastronomy: "I've learned to appreciate quality. I don't allow myself to eat anything that is less than the best...." After listening for several minutes, Mom turned to me and said, "Oh come off it—you've always been a picky eater!"

My mother was telling the truth. Of the six children in my family, I was the most difficult to feed. My prejudices went way beyond the don't-let-the-peas-touch-the-mashed-potatoes school of fussiness. I remember coming home from school every day and asking my mother the classic question, "What's for dinner?" Almost before she could get the answer out of her mouth, my knee-jerk response was, "I don't like it." I was every home cook's worst nightmare.

Flash forward to four years ago, when I was pregnant. Someone gave me a copy of Dr. Spock's book *Feeding Your Baby and Child* (written thirty-five years ago). Dipping into it, I ran across a paragraph that made me start with recognition: "A strange fact but true is that a parent who has been a feeding problem in his or her own childhood is especially tempted to urge and force feedings, even though he knows consciously that this will work in the wrong direction."

After giving considerable thought to these practical and psychological stumbling blocks, I decided that the best way to nurture Simon's body and his taste buds was to plan a widely varied diet—it's the best way to keep fit and find physical well-being, not to mention beginning a lifetime of appreciating sophisticated flavors. But try explaining that to a three-year-old (or a five-year-old, or a seven-year-old—or even a twenty-five-year-old, for that matter).

So my way of working around Simon's natural predilections has been to use my skill and experience with food to come up with lots of delicious, fun recipes that contain a variety of ingredients he might not otherwise eat. I also want the recipes to be relatively easy, knowing that I won't be able to spend hours in the kitchen for *anyone,* including Simon, except on special occasions.

As much as possible, by the way, the recipes are scaled down to avoid making too much food if you're cooking for a small family or feeding only one or two children separately from adults. Then, if you want to increase the amount to feed more people, or to freeze extras, I've marked those recipes that can easily be doubled or tripled.

If you are feeding children and grown-ups at the same time, there is often a conflict between the low-fat, low-cholesterol requirements of adults and the high-calorie needs of children. With few exceptions, children need food densely packed with calories in order to grow and develop properly, and that usually means food that is "fattening" for their parents. In order to help you find a happy medium, I have given some low-fat alternatives to ingredients in some of the recipes, so you can decide which version best suits your family's needs.

Whenever possible, I have given volume yields rather than portion sizes—which are arbitrary in the best cookbooks. Only you know, by the age of your child, his temperament, and his mood, how much he might eat at a meal. You can easily figure out—from the yield I have provided—how many of *your* child's portions each recipe will make.

As you'll see on the following pages, I've found ways to give Simon a more varied and nutritious diet than he might have had otherwise, and I've assuaged my worry about the food he eats. He benefits, and so do

I. Now, if he wants a hot dog from the street, that's fine; if he eats three pieces of birthday cake at a party, that's okay, too. Now that I'm less anxious about the food Simon eats day in and day out, there's room for some junk food as well.

Mainly, I've eliminated a major source of confrontation between me and my son, and isn't that one of the goals of raising children? He's happy, I'm happy, and I hope that this book will bring the kind of happiness into the lives of you and your child(ren) that we experience three times a day at our table. With kisses from Simon and me, we give you our first joint venture.

A NOTE ABOUT THE GENDER IN THIS BOOK

I am well aware that the current style is to use the female gender when writing books about children, in order to counteract the effects of previous generations when little girls were peremptorily overlooked by authors. Since my child is a boy I always think in terms of "he," and so have used the male gender exclusively—not because of any anti-feminist tendencies, but simply because when I think of feeding a little one, it's a "him" that comes to mind.

GRAPHIC SYMBOLS

 CAN BE MADE IN 30 MINUTES OR LESS

 CAN BE DOUBLED OR TRIPLED

 CAN BE FROZEN (UP TO TWO MONTHS)

 FOR GROWN-UPS, TOO

 GOOD FOR BABIES, TOO (the food may need to be pureed, depending on the age of your baby)

HINTS FOR FEEDING INFANTS AND TODDLERS

From a Mother and Son
Who Have Survived Those Stages

I started to write this book when Simon was just beginning to eat solid food, when he was about seven months old. The months ahead seemed daunting because Simon is my first child and I had never fed a baby before (for more than a meal at a time!). I didn't know what foods to give him, when to introduce them, or how much he should eat.

After his first birthday, however, I realized that those first few months of solid food are really training—for both the parents and the child—and not nutritionally significant. The baby is getting used to eating, and the parents are getting used to feeding him, while almost all of the nourishment in the baby's diet comes from the milk he is drinking. The amount or type of solid food a baby eats before he is a year old—within reason—is less important than new mothers think. In any event, he will "tell" you when he's had enough, or too much, or the wrong kind or consistency of food. (It's really one of the first times a parent learns that there's no forcing a child to do anything he doesn't want to.) The task is made much simpler by the fact that so-called single generation baby foods in jars—a puree of one ingredient with nothing else added—are excellent these days (and some are even made from organic fruits and vegetables). Many brands don't contain salt or sugar or fillers, or anything else that will corrupt nascent taste buds.

After a baby gets a few more teeth (at about twelve or fourteen months), he can chew food with a little texture to it: ground rather than pureed. One of the best gifts I ever received when Simon was that age was the Happy Baby Food Mill, which is a miniature food mill, the most efficient piece of equipment in my kitchen. It grinds an ounce or two of adult table food to the proper consistency for an infant to chew; this simple item (which sells for just a few dollars) makes the prospect of feeding a toddler a cinch. With this food mill and all the recipes in this book marked for babies, you should be able to get through the toddler stage with little or no anxiety.

Having said this, however, I am sure that you are like I was and are still worried about the *details* of feeding a baby, especially if you've never done it before. You should discuss all of your concerns with your pediatrician. And, for further assistance through the baby and toddler periods, I offer the following bits of advice that I learned the hard way.

FOOD TIPS

■ Avocado and banana are the two foods that can be given raw to a baby in the first year. They should be very ripe and mashed with a little formula.

Hints for Feeding Infants and Toddlers

■ To make your own oatmeal cereal for a young baby, place rolled oats in a blender or food processor and reduce it to powder; then cook it with milk, water, or formula until it reaches the proper consistency.

■ Cream of brown rice cereal (sold in health food stores) is a good alternative to the cream of wheat and cream of rice that I grew up with, which taste more like library paste than food. Whole grain *instant* baby cereal, also sold in health food stores, is best for babies who are under one year old. The commercial varieties contain iron, which young babies need, so if you go the whole grain route you might ask your doctor for a type of liquid baby vitamin that contains iron, as I did.

■ Babies less than one year old can't digest uncooked apples, but applesauce is ideal at this age, since it's low in citric acid (which can cause allergic reactions) and high in vitamin E. Peel and core an apple and cut it into small chunks; cook it over low heat, covered, with 2 tablespoons of water until soft and mushy. Mash with a fork or put into a blender or food processor to puree completely. Serve the cooked apple as is, or blend it with cereal, yogurt, or cottage cheese. Pears can be prepared in exactly the same way.

■ As unlikely as it sounds, young babies often love to eat grapefruit. Cut a wedge of grapefruit (leaving the skin on); if he's too young to hold it himself, you can hold the fruit side up to his mouth and watch him suck and chew contentedly for minutes.

■ When I was pregnant with Simon, I read in Dr. Spock that a baby will accept milk that is cold, room temperature, or warm, depending on what is given from the beginning. I took this advice to heart, and we have been living by it ever since. When Simon was on formula (and later on goat's milk, since he was allergic to cow's milk as an infant), he drank it at room temperature if it was straight from the can, or sometimes cold if it was made with powder and refrigerated. He never refused it at either temperature. When he began to eat solid food, I never warmed his pureed fruits or vegetables, but served them to him at room temperature. He still eats his food at room temperature, except if something is freshly made and warm from the oven or stove. This also happens to be the way I prefer to eat, since food that is very hot or very cold loses some of its taste; food is most flavorful when it is closest to room temperature.

■ When Simon was about nine months old, all he wanted to eat was cereal, so I got around that obsession by mixing instant brown rice cereal with jars of pureed vegetables or fruit, in a half-and-half proportion (without adding extra liquid), and he happily gobbled it up.

■ Lamb is the meat least likely to cause an allergic reaction in babies, so it's a good choice for introducing meat to a baby's diet.

■ The safest way to enlarge the hole in a rubber nipple is to put a wooden toothpick in the hole and boil the nipple for five minutes; remove the toothpick when it cools.
The most expedient way to enlarge the hole in a bottle's nipple is to stick a sharp knife point into the existing hole and pierce the rubber until a small slit is made.

■ Offer new foods to a baby at the beginning of a meal, when he is hungriest and more likely to accept a new taste.

■ Frozen peas are soothing to gums that are inflamed and sore from teething—and they're fun to eat.

■ Use pre-cooked, dry baby cereal in place of flour to coat foods, such as pieces of fish or chicken, before sautéing. It adds an extra bit of enrichment and a delicious flavor.

■ Piles of finely shredded vegetables are fun for a young baby to play with *and* to eat—and much safer than sticks or cubes of raw vegetables that might get stuck in his throat and induce choking. You might try carrots, turnips, kohlrabi, or seeded and peeled cucumbers.

Hints for Feeding Infants and Toddlers

■ While toddlers usually love soup, they have a hard time getting it from the bowl to their mouths without spilling. If your family is having soup, strain out the solids—vegetables, noodles, and meat—from your baby's portion and serve them to him to pick up with his fingers or a spoon. Put the cooled broth in a cup to drink.

■ If you have some jars of pureed fruit or vegetables left over from when your baby was smaller, use them up by stirring them into cottage cheese or yogurt and serving them for breakfast or a snack (be sure to check the expiration date on the jar).

■ Eggs can cause an allergic reaction in babies who are younger than one year old, so you shouldn't feed them to a baby until he passes his first birthday. (It's the egg whites that are usually the culprit, but it's best to stay away from eggs altogether until later.)
A more serious problem for babies who are younger than one year old is infant botulism, which is caused by eating honey that contains *botulinum* spores. Honey should be avoided until a baby's second year. (You can substitute sugar or syrup in recipes that call for honey.)

■ Michele Urvater, author of *Cooking the Nouvelle Cuisine in America,* has an eight-year-old daughter who has been a picky eater since early on. But when she was about a year old, she loved to eat a puree her mother made from the meat, vegetables, and broth of the stockpot. Michele usually made this puree in batches and froze it in ice cube trays for later meals.

■ The arrowroot cookies sold in health food stores are easy for very young babies to digest, and are made with fruit juice rather than sugar.

■ Corn puffs are a godsend for tiny children, who like to chew on light, airy, crunchy things. The same goes for Oatios and Nature Os, two health-food brands of cereal that are like Cheerios, only made with whole grains and without added sugar.

■ Whole wheat teething biscuits, which are sold in health food stores, are as dark and hard as dog biscuits, and Simon loved them when he was teething. Also, they don't disintegrate as fast as the supermarket brands.

■ When he was about eighteen months old, Simon wanted to eat everything by himself with a fork—including tofu cubes and pieces of fruit. I found that a little oyster fork was just the right size for his hands and mouth; it was even better than the forks made especially for babies.

Since he also wanted to learn to use a spoon at about this age, I gave him soft tofu in a bowl, which he could spoon up by himself quite easily.

FEEDING TIPS

■ During the winter, when a baby's chin and cheeks tend to become chapped, spread a little petroleum jelly on his face before a meal, so the food that ends up all over those tender areas will wipe off easily.

■ The hard, fibrous core of a pineapple is soothing to a baby who's teething. If you cut the core lengthwise into sticks, they're easy to hold.

■ Dr. Spock recommends using a clean wooden tongue depressor for a baby's first feedings. Available at any drugstore, they're much more efficient than even a demitasse spoon, at least until your baby can sit up for his food.

When your baby is eight or nine months old, plastic spoons are most practical. The elongated shape is perfect for a tiny mouth, and the plastic is not as harsh as metal on tender, teething gums.

■ Here's an excellent snack or dinner-time treat for a teething baby: cook a chicken thigh (broil it or bake it, or simmer it in soup), then trim off almost all the meat and make sure to remove the gristle at both ends of the bone. Give the bone to the baby for many minutes of chewing pleasure, plus a bit of protein as well.

■ For very young babies, leftovers should be kept for no more than two days. After that time, harmful bacteria can multiply quickly. Toddlers can tolerate food that's been refrigerated a bit longer.

■ Babies' bottles should be heated in the microwave oven with caution. You run the danger of assuming that the milk or formula is the right temperature because the bottle doesn't feel hot, while the liquid inside is scalding.

■ Those plastic drinking cups with snap-on lids are essential, but they are *not* spillproof, as anyone knows who has watched a baby flail one. The kind that makes the least mess has holes only on one side for drinking, rather than drinking holes on one side and an air hole on the other side of the lid.

■ Two rubber bands, placed about an inch apart on a drinking cup, give a baby a good grip and help to prevent accidents.

■ Buy sturdy plastic or coated-paper disposable bowls, sold in the supermarket, for your baby's mealtimes. They won't crack or break if they're pushed off a table, plus you can throw them away. Make sure they're microwavable if you plan to heat foods in them.

■ To clean a high chair easily in the summer, put it outside and spray it with a garden hose; in the winter, put it under the shower and spray hot water on it for a few minutes.

■ A small sponge placed in the pocket of a plastic bib will keep it open wide enough to catch *all* the spills and drips.

■ A rubber nonslip dish mat placed on the bottom of a high chair or on a grown-up chair will help prevent a child from sliding down.

SOUPS

Soup is a great way to get vegetables into a child who normally won't touch them, and to introduce him to new flavors. (A sneaky soup trick I learned from Jane Brody is to make soup with the vegetables that your children don't like and puree it, then add little cubes of the vegetables that your children like.) At first I resisted the idea because I thought soup would be messy for Simon to eat, but my wiser friends pointed out that preparing and eating soup can become a warming family ritual, and they were right.

22-BITE CHOWDER

Makes about 5 cups

I developed this soup-stew in my never-ending campaign to find ways to cook fish that Simon likes. When I first presented it to him, he had a box of raisins in one hand and was not about to try the chowder. After I coaxed a bite into his mouth, he forgot about the raisins and finished two helpings of soup, so his daddy coined this name for the dish. George and I ate big, steaming bowls of the same chowder for dinner, along with pilot crackers and a salad, and we were just as happy as Simon.

2 strips bacon

1 tablespoon olive oil

¾ cup minced onion

1 garlic clove, minced

1 tablespoon all-purpose flour

4 cups chicken broth

1 large or 2 medium potatoes, peeled and cut into ¼-inch
        cubes

½ teaspoon dried thyme *or* fresh thyme leaves

½ teaspoon salt

Freshly ground pepper to taste (white pepper, if you
        have it)

1 pound flounder fillets (see Hint), cut into ½-inch cubes

1 cup milk

A Way Around the Ultimate Picky Eater

My friend Nina Zagat has two boys, and her eleven-year-old, John, is the pickier eater. She copes with his fussiness by asking him to write "John's Delicious List" from time to time, and it's posted on the refrigerator for everyone (mother, father, older brother, babysitter) to refer to when making meals for him. On the list are all the foods that John likes, in every category—vegetables, fruit, meat, snacks, and so on—so no one can make a mistake.

1. In a large saucepan, cook the bacon over medium heat for 5 minutes, turning to crisp on both sides. Drain the bacon on a paper towel, leaving the drippings in the pan.

2. Add the olive oil to the pan and sauté the onion and garlic over medium heat for 5 minutes. Sprinkle in the flour and stir to blend thoroughly; cook for 30 seconds. Pour in the chicken broth, bring to a boil, and reduce the heat so the liquid simmers slowly.

3. Add the potatoes, thyme, salt, and pepper and simmer for 15 minutes, uncovered, stirring occasionally. Stir in the fish cubes and milk and simmer for 10 minutes, uncovered, stirring occasionally. Taste for seasoning. Serve when cool enough to eat. Crumble the cooked bacon pieces and sprinkle over the top of the chowder before serving.

Hint: You can use any kind of mild-tasting fish fillets, such as sole or whitefish. Frozen fish fillets that have been defrosted and cut into cubes are okay, too, since texture isn't as much of an issue here as it is for broiled or sautéed fish.

To reduce the cholesterol content: Some form of bacon is traditional in most chowders, but if you'd rather not use it, you can substitute 1 tablespoon of olive oil (raising the total to 2 tablespoons) for the bacon drippings.

Storage: This chowder will keep for 5 days in the refrigerator.

X2

1-2-3 PEA SOUP

Makes 2½ cups

Because of the combination of rice and peas, this soup is a complete protein source—just as nutritious as beef or chicken, without the fat and cholesterol that comes with meat. I gave it this title because it's easy to put together.

This is a delicious soup for the whole family. We like to serve it as a main course from a tureen, accompanied by a wedge of sharp cheddar cheese and a loaf of pumpernickel bread.

It also makes an ideal cold soup for hot summer days. Serve chilled, and top with plain yogurt or sour cream, and perhaps a sprig of dill for garnish. You can also stir together yogurt and milk in equal proportions to drizzle over the top of the soup in the style of a Jackson Pollack painting or in a happy face design.

½ cup yellow or green split peas
2 tablespoons brown *or* white rice
2½ cups water
1 small onion *or* ½ medium onion
1 medium carrot, peeled
1 celery stalk
½ teaspoon salt
Freshly ground pepper to taste
½ bay leaf

For an Upset Tummy

■ **If your child is nauseated, weak mint tea mixed with a little honey might settle his stomach. Mint contains magnesium, which is found in many over-the-counter digestive aids that are unsuitable for children.**

■ **A bout of gas can often be calmed by chamomile tea or fennel tea.**

1. Put the split peas, rice, and water into a medium, heavy pot and bring to a boil; reduce the heat to low.

2. Cut the onion, carrot, and celery into large chunks and put into a food processor; process until the vegetables are finely chopped.

3. Add the vegetables to the pot along with the salt, pepper, and bay leaf. Simmer, covered, for 1 hour, stirring occasionally. Remove the bay leaf and discard.

4. Puree the soup in a food processor. (This last step is not essential if you're in a rush.) Correct the seasoning and serve when cool enough to eat.

Variations: Make the soup richer by using chicken or beef broth instead of water, or a combination of broth and water. You can also substitute tomato juice for half the liquid.

You can vary the seasonings as much as you like. Some possible additions to add at the beginning of the cooking time are ¼ teaspoon ground cumin, for a southwestern flavor; 1 tablespoon dried mushrooms; or 1 teaspoon tomato paste. Add 1 tablespoon chopped fresh parsley or other fresh herbs after the soup is cooked and pureed.

Storage: This will keep in the refrigerator for up to 1 week.

❄ **X2** 🚶 👶

Soups

ELIZABETH ANDOH'S THICK WHITE NOODLES IN EGG DROP SOUP (Tamago Toji Udon)

Makes 3 to 4 servings

Elizabeth Andoh, author of At Home with Japanese Cooking *and* An American Taste of Japan, *and her daughter Rena call this recipe "the all-time winner for tiny taste buds." Elizabeth adds, "Making the noodles from scratch becomes a wonderful rainy day activity when the park is off limits." Your child can get indoor exercise by stamping on the noodle dough to "knead" it.*

NOODLES

2 tablespoons salt

¾ cup warm water

2 cups all-purpose unbleached flour, plus 1 cup additional
for hands, board, rolling pin

1 cup bread flour

BROTH

5 to 6 inches *kombu* (dried kelp)

5 cups cold water

2 (5-gram) packets *or* ½ cup *katsuo bushi* (loose fish
flakes)

⅓ cup *usukuchi shoyu* (light soy sauce imported from
Japan)

⅓ cup *mirin* (syrupy rice wine)

White part of 2 scallions

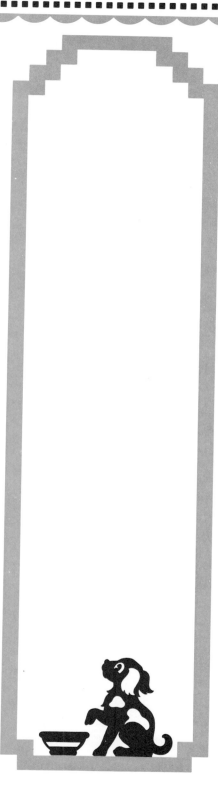

GARNISH

1 egg, beaten
Green tops of 2 scallions, minced

1. *To make the noodles:* In a small bowl, mix the salt with the warm water and dissolve.

2. In a large bowl, stir the 2 cups all-purpose flour with the 1 cup bread flour.

3. Pour half the saltwater over the flour mixture and fold in with your hand. Gradually add more water, a few drops at a time, just until the dough stays together and can be shaped into 2 or 3 balls. Wrap each ball in a plastic bag and close securely. Let the dough rest for 10 minutes.

4. Lightly flour a sheet of sturdy plastic (see Hints) and place one of the balls of dough on it. Dust the dough with flour, then cover with a second sheet of plastic.

Here comes the fun part: Place the dough on a carpeted area and stamp on it with your whole foot, not just heel. When the dough is flattened out, lift off the top sheet of plastic, fold the dough into a ball again, and repeat. Stamp and fold several times until the dough is smooth and satiny. Set aside and repeat this procedure with remaining balls of dough.

5. Transfer the satiny dough to a lightly floured surface and roll into a large oval about ⅛ inch thick. Dust the dough sheet with flour, fan-fold, and cut into ¼-inch-thick ribbons. Repeat this procedure with the remaining sheets of dough.

(continued on next page)

Soups

6. Bring a large pot of water to a rolling boil. Shake off the excess flour from the noodles and boil them, one batch at a time, for 6 to 8 minutes. The noodles should be tender but not mushy. Drain and rinse under cold water to wash off the excess starch. (Most children like luke-warm food, so when you put the cold noodles into the hot broth, they will be just perfect. But if you like your noodles hot, do a final rinse under boiling water just before putting them into the soup.)

7. *To make the broth:* Place the *kombu* in a pot with the cold water and bring to a boil.

8. Remove and discard the *kombu.* Sprinkle 1 packet or half the *katsuo bushi* over the broth. Wait 3 minutes, stir, and strain the broth through a strainer lined with filter paper. Discard the flakes and filter.

9. Season the broth with the *usukuchi shoyu, mirin,* and white part of scallions. Simmer for 5 minutes, remove from the heat, and sprinkle the remaining *katsuo bushi* over the broth. Strain the broth through a strainer lined with filter paper. Discard the filter and its contents.

10. *To assemble the soup:* Place the noodles in the bottom of individual bowls.

11. Bring the broth to a boil. Stir the broth in a clockwise direction. Pour in the beaten egg and stir in a counterclockwise direction.

12. Remove the broth from the heat and pour over the noodles. Garnish with minced scallion greens.

Yes, You Can Play with Your Food

■ If you're serving soup or stew to a child, you can make it fun by letting him write his name on top, using yogurt. Thin a little plain yogurt by stirring in some milk, and give the child a demitasse spoon to dip into the yogurt and use as a "pencil."

■ To decorate a casserole, "draw" a face or some other decoration on the top with strips of cheese and/or vegetables before baking. An older child can take on this project himself.

Note: The broth can be prepared several days in advance and refrigerated.

This soup can be made with either homemade or good-quality canned chicken broth, if you don't want to go to the trouble of making a Japanese broth.

Hints: You can buy the sturdy plastic sheets used to make the noodles in a dime store—you'll need 2 yards, cut in half, to make at least two 30-inch squares. When you're finished, just wipe sheets with a damp cloth or sponge. To store for future use, lay a towel (paper or cloth) between the 2 sheets before folding.

The Japanese ingredients in this recipe can be purchased from stores that specialize in Japanese foods; or you can buy the ingredients mail order from Katagiri, 224 East 59th Street, New York, N.Y. 10022; (212) 755-3566.

X2 🚶 👶

MADGE ROSENBERG'S SOUP FOR A WINTER DAY

Makes 6 servings

Madge Rosenberg is the owner of Soutine Bakery in New York City, and the mother of three children. For years, she taught a cooking class to children, and the following recipe is from that class. She says, "This is one of the kids' favorites to make as well as to eat."

6 beef bones
3 quarts water
2 celery stalks
2 medium carrots
6 peppercorns
1½ teaspoons salt
1 bay leaf
½ teaspoon dried thyme
1 garlic clove
1 cup barley
6 cups chopped vegetables, in ½-inch dice (carrots, green
     beans, turnips, potatoes, tomatoes, leeks,
     mushrooms, zucchini)
1 cup drained canned chickpeas

1. In a 400°F. oven, brown the beef bones for 15 to 30 minutes, or until brown all over.

2. Place the bones in a very large soup pot. Add the water, celery, carrots, peppercorns, salt, bay leaf, thyme, and garlic. Bring to a boil and simmer, partly covered, for 1½ hours. Strain the broth through cheesecloth or a clean dish towel, remove the grease (see Note), and return the broth to the pot.

3. Add the barley; bring the broth to a boil, lower the heat to a simmer, and cook for 30 minutes. Add the chopped vegetables according to cooking time; fast-cooking vegetables such as tomatoes and zucchini should be added last. Simmer until the vegetables are cooked, about 30 minutes. Add the chickpeas, simmer for 5 more minutes, and serve when cool enough to eat.

Note: You can prepare the soup through step 2 and refrigerate the broth after straining it; after a few hours, or overnight, the fat will have hardened on top and will be easier to remove.

Storage: The finished soup will keep in the refrigerator for up to a week; bring to a hard boil before serving it again.

❄ **X2** 👨 🍼

MINESTRONE SEMIFREDDO

Makes about 10 cups

In Italy in the summertime, thick vegetable soup is served at room temperature, thus this Italian name which translates as "cool vegetable soup." It's thick enough to stay on a spoon being wielded by a small hand.

Instead of pasta or rice, this version is made with egg noodles that are formed in the shapes of the letters of the alphabet (you can find them in the pasta section of your supermarket). Once they are old enough, children love to hunt for letters floating in their soup.

Grown-ups might like to make their soup more bracing with the addition of pesto (recipe follows).

2 tablespoons olive oil
½ cup minced onion
2 garlic cloves, minced
½ cup diced carrot
½ cup diced celery
6 cups chicken broth
1 cup peeled diced potato
½ cup diced green beans
1 cup drained canned tomatoes, chopped
½ cup alphabet pasta
½ teaspoon salt
1 cup finely shredded Savoy or regular green cabbage
½ cup frozen green peas, thawed
1 cup drained canned white beans
¼ cup minced fresh basil *or* parsley leaves
½ cup grated Parmesan cheese

Simon Soup

When we come home late and it's time for a quick dinner before bed, I make Simon a soup-cereal by mixing a handful of oatmeal into chicken broth and cooking it over low heat until it's reached a creamy consistency, then I add a bit of grated cheese. If I have some on hand, I mix in a bit of frozen corn when I add the oatmeal.

1. In a large saucepan, heat the oil over medium heat and sauté the onion and garlic for 4 minutes, or until the onion is transparent.

2. Add the carrot and celery and cook for 5 minutes, covered, stirring occasionally. Add the broth and bring to a boil. Add the potato, green beans, tomatoes, pasta, and salt. Reduce the heat to medium and simmer for 7 to 10 minutes.

3. Add the cabbage, peas, beans, and herb. Cook for 3 more minutes. Stir in the Parmesan cheese. Taste for seasoning, and serve when cool enough to eat, or let come to room temperature before serving.

Variation: If you have the rind of a piece of cheese, you can add it whole to the soup along with the broth, to give the soup a rich, cheesy flavor. In that case, omit the salt and the Parmesan, remove the cheese rind before serving, and taste the soup for seasoning at the end of the cooking time, in case it needs some additional salt.

Storage: The soup will keep in the refrigerator for up to 1 week.

❄ **X2** 🚶

PESTO

You might like to heighten the flavor of Minestrone Semi-freddo (page 34) or any other vegetable soup with the addition of pesto, which is served at the table—each diner stirs in as much as he or she likes.

2 cups fresh basil leaves
¾ cup olive oil
3 tablespoons pine nuts (pignoli)
3 garlic cloves
1 teaspoon salt
¾ cup grated Parmesan cheese

Put all ingredients in a blender or food processor and process until mixture is pureed.

Storage: If you pour a thin layer of oil on the top of it, pesto will keep in the refrigerator for up to a month. You can freeze pesto in an airtight container for up to 6 months, digging out a frozen tablespoonful when you need it for soup or for flavoring pasta sauce.

Always Prepared

Carry two clothespins in your purse so that when you go to a restaurant without a bib you can clip a grownup napkin to the shoulders of your child's shirt to protect his clothes.

MISO SOUP

Makes about 2¼ cups

This is similar to the popular soup you get in Japanese restaurants; in Japan it's eaten for breakfast. The key ingredient is miso, a sweet-salty bean paste made from soybeans, that is not only tasty but also very nutritious. The texture of miso, by the way, is not unlike refrigerated cookie dough.

2 cups chicken broth
2 teaspoons miso (available in plastic containers in health
     food stores and Oriental groceries)
1 cup diced tofu

1. Bring the chicken broth to a boil. Reduce the heat so the broth simmers.

2. Add 1 tablespoon hot broth to the miso in a small bowl and blend into a smooth paste. Add the miso paste and tofu to the broth; stir to blend. Serve when cool enough to eat.

Variations: You can also add vegetables, such as thin carrot rounds or sliced mushrooms, or cooked noodles to this soup. Health food stores sell many different kinds of dried seaweed, and you might like to try one in this soup. I like *nijiki.*

Storage: This soup will keep about 2 days in the refrigerator.

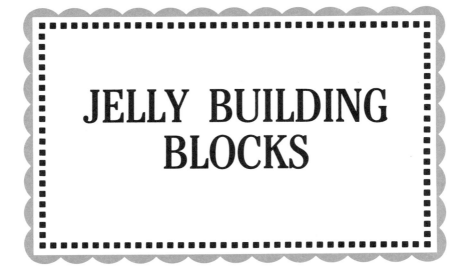

JELLY BUILDING BLOCKS

These jelly squares are perfect for kids of all ages: the tiniest baby, just beginning to eat solid food; the hungry toddler looking for a nutritious snack; even the older kid who likes "fun food" (he can help you cut them out with cookie cutters).

When Simon was about a year old, he refused to eat almost anything other than tofu squares, so I devised these protein and vegetable blocks to give some variety to his diet. The texture was similar to tofu, and he loved to pick up the squares with his fingers.

Now that he's older, he still enjoys eating them—and he enjoys making them with me as well; the recipes are simple enough for him to participate.

Relief from Canker Sores

If your child is prone to painful canker sores, he should stay away from all nuts and seeds (including peanut butter and coconut), as well as chocolate.

Jelly Building Blocks

BASIC BLOCKS

Makes about 6 dozen 1-inch blocks

3 cups cold juice (see Note)
3 packets unflavored gelatin
2 tablespoons sugar *or* honey (optional)

1. Bring 1½ cups of the juice to a boil.

2. While the juice is heating, sprinkle the gelatin over the remaining 1½ cups juice. Let stand for 1 minute. Add the hot juice and stir until gelatin is completely dissolved. Stir in the optional sugar or honey.

3. Pour into an 8- or 9-inch square baking pan. Refrigerate until set, at least 3 hours. Cut into 1-inch squares.

Note: Some suggestions for the liquid in this recipe are organic apple juice, white or purple grape juice, orange juice, grapefruit juice, unsweetened cranberry juice (available in health food stores, but since it's a bit sour, you'll need to add the honey or sugar for sweetening), tomato juice, V-8 juice.

Variation: You can also add one of the following after the gelatin is dissolved: unsweetened coconut (found in health food stores), cut-up strawberries, pitted cherries, or bits of peeled apple.

Storage: These squares will last for about 1 week in your refrigerator.

 X2

AVOCADO BLOCKS

Makes about 6 dozen 1-inch blocks

The California Avocado Commission sent me this recipe when they found out I was writing a book on cooking for children. I feel that Americans should feed more avocados to their children and babies, since they're so practical and nutritious. (Avocados contain more potassium than bananas, for example). Several mothers in Brazil told me that avocado is the first food they feed their babies, just as we usually feed our tiny babies mashed bananas.

1 (6-ounce) can frozen orange juice concentrate, thawed
¼ cup cold water
2 packets unflavored gelatin
⅓ cup ripe avocado chunks
1 cup boiling water

1. Combine the orange juice concentrate and water in a bowl and sprinkle the gelatin over the liquid. Let stand for 1 minute.

2. Pour this mixture into a blender and add the avocado chunks; blend until very smooth. Pour boiling water into the blender and blend again until smooth.

3. Pour into an 8- or 9-inch square baking pan. Refrigerate until set, at least 3 hours. Cut into 1-inch squares.

Storage: These squares will last for about 1 week in your refrigerator.

Frozen Fun

■ Children who won't eat certain fruits will sometimes like them if they are frozen in some form.

■ Blend strawberries, melon chunks, and/or bananas in a blender with evaporated milk, pour the mixture into a popsicle mold, and freeze; you will have healthful homemade snacks. (You can also make these successfully with fresh milk, if you'd rather.)

■ If your child is feverish or has the flu, a fruit juice popsicle might be soothing. You can buy plastic molds, or you can make your own by using small paper cups and wooden tongue depressors or plastic spoons as handles. Freeze the juice until solid and peel off the paper to eat.

■ You can freeze fruit juice in an ice cube tray and give the cubes to your child one by one to suck on. These are especially welcome to a child who has a sore throat. Keep a batch of these fruit juice cubes in the freezer to have on hand when your child falls down and gets a fat lip—it will soothe the hurt.

■ Make a frozen yogurt popsicle by stirring yogurt vigorously until it is thin, pouring it into a small paper cup, and putting in a wooden tongue depressor or plastic spoon for a handle. Freeze until solid and peel off the paper cup to eat.

Jelly Building Blocks

CARROT BLOCKS

Makes about 6 dozen 1-inch blocks

1 pound carrots, peeled, trimmed, and cut into 1-inch
    pieces
3 cups cold carrot juice (see Hint)
3 packets unflavored gelatin

1. Cook carrots in 1½ cups of the carrot juice and enough water to cover over medium-low heat for 35 to 40 minutes, or until tender when pierced with a fork.

2. Meanwhile, sprinkle the gelatin over the remaining 1½ cups carrot juice and let stand for 1 minute. When the carrots are cooked, drain off all but 1½ cups of the hot liquid. Put the cooked carrots with this liquid into a food processor and process until pureed. (The remaining liquid can be used for soup.)

3. Add the gelatin mixture to the carrot puree and process again until well mixed. Pour into an 8- or 9-inch square baking pan. Refrigerate until set, at least 3 hours. Cut into 1-inch squares.

Hint: You can find unadulterated carrot juice in cans in the supermarket, or you can make it yourself in a home juicer.

Storage: These squares will last for about 1 week in your refrigerator.

X2 🛒

CHICKEN BLOCKS

Makes about 6 dozen 1-inch blocks

4 ounces boneless and skinless chicken breast (about ½
    chicken breast)
1 (14½-ounce) can chicken broth
3 packets unflavored gelatin
1½ cups cold V-8 juice

1. Poach the chicken in the broth over medium-high
heat for 15 minutes, or until cooked through.

2. While the chicken is poaching, sprinkle the gelatin
over the V-8 juice and let stand for 1 minute.

3. Put the cooked chicken and hot chicken broth into a
food processor or blender and process until pureed. Add
the juice and gelatin mixture and process until well
mixed. Pour into an 8- or 9-inch square baking pan. Refrigerate until set, at least 3 hours. Cut into 1-inch
squares.

Storage: These squares will last for about 1 week in your
refrigerator.

🔳 **X2** 👶

To Help the Medicine Go Down

If a child balks when you try to give him liquid medicine, chill the medicine first and the taste won't be as strong.

MUFFIN MEALS

The idea for these muffin meals came about when I first considered making a meat loaf for Simon. Even though meat loaf is a convenient way to feed protein and vitamins to a growing child, a slice from a big loaf of meat seemed too unwieldy, so I decided to make some Simon-size loaves in a muffin tin. The portion size was perfect, and he was delighted with his own muffin, so I continued developing recipes for the same format. When I'm in a hurry to fix him dinner, I pull one of these out of the freezer and defrost it in the microwave. We also pack them in Simon's lunch box, to eat for school, picnic, and playground lunches.

SALMON MUFFIN MEAL

Makes 6 muffin-size loaves

1 (6½-ounce) can skinless and boneless salmon (do not
    drain)
2 eggs
½ cup coarsely chopped celery
½ cup quick-cooking rolled oats
¼ teaspoon baking powder
¼ cup evaporated milk
2 teaspoons fresh lemon juice
¾ teaspoon salt
¼ teaspoon ground pepper
2 dashes Tabasco

1. Preheat the oven to 350°F. Coat 6 cups of a standard
muffin tin with nonstick baking spray.

2. Put all the ingredients into the bowl of a food processor and process until pureed. Spoon an equal amount of
the salmon mixture into each of the cups. Bake for 30
minutes, or until firm to the touch and light golden brown.
Unmold and serve when cool enough to eat, or refrigerate
and serve cold.

Variations: You can substitute canned tuna for the
canned salmon.
    You can also bake the mixture in a 9 x 5-inch loaf pan
for 30 to 40 minutes, until light brown.

Storage: These muffins will keep for about 1 week in the
refrigerator.

❄ **X2** ⵙ

VEGGIE MUFFIN MEAL

Makes 3 muffin-size loaves

The nuts, milk, and egg supply the protein in these little muffins, and the carrots round out the nutrition.

½ cup fresh whole wheat or white bread crumbs
⅓ cup grated carrot
⅓ cup ground nuts, such as walnuts, peanuts, pecans
¼ cup milk
2 tablespoons minced onion
2 tablespoons minced fresh parsley
2 teaspoons honey
2 teaspoons reduced-sodium soy sauce
1 egg yolk

1. Preheat the oven to 350°F. Coat 3 cups of a standard muffin tin with nonstick baking spray.

2. Mix all the ingredients and spoon equal amounts into the muffin tin. Bake for 25 minutes, or until firm to the touch and light golden brown. Unmold and serve when cool enough to eat, or refrigerate and serve cold.

Variations: Any other grated vegetable can be used: kohlrabi, parsnips, summer squash—even potatoes.

You can also bake the mixture in a 9 x 5-inch loaf pan, leaving it in the oven long enough to become firm and light golden brown, about 30 minutes. Serve in slices.

Storage: These muffins will keep for about 1 week in the refrigerator.

❄ **X2** 🚶

HAM-ON-RYE MUFFIN MEAL

Makes 6 muffin-size loaves

8 ounces boiled ham, cut into chunks
1½ slices rye bread, crusts removed, torn into pieces
2 tablespoons fresh parsley leaves
2 tablespoons minced scallion greens
1 egg yolk
1 tablespoon unsweetened apricot jam
1 teaspoon honey mustard (see Hint)

1. Preheat the oven to 375°F. Coat 6 cups of a standard muffin tin with nonstick baking spray.

2. Put all the ingredients except the mustard in the bowl of a food processor and process until completely ground. Spoon an equal amount of the ground mixture into each of the cups. Bake for 30 minutes.

3. Remove the muffin tin from the oven and pat the excess drippings from the tops of the muffins with a paper towel. Brush the top of each muffin with the mustard, return to the oven, and bake for 5 more minutes. Unmold and serve when cool enough to eat, or refrigerate and serve cold.

VEGGIE MUFFIN MEAL

Makes 3 muffin-size loaves

The nuts, milk, and egg supply the protein in these little muffins, and the carrots round out the nutrition.

½ cup fresh whole wheat or white bread crumbs
⅓ cup grated carrot
⅓ cup ground nuts, such as walnuts, peanuts, pecans
¼ cup milk
2 tablespoons minced onion
2 tablespoons minced fresh parsley
2 teaspoons honey
2 teaspoons reduced-sodium soy sauce
1 egg yolk

1. Preheat the oven to 350°F. Coat 3 cups of a standard muffin tin with nonstick baking spray.

2. Mix all the ingredients and spoon equal amounts into the muffin tin. Bake for 25 minutes, or until firm to the touch and light golden brown. Unmold and serve when cool enough to eat, or refrigerate and serve cold.

Variations: Any other grated vegetable can be used: kohlrabi, parsnips, summer squash—even potatoes.

You can also bake the mixture in a 9 x 5-inch loaf pan, leaving it in the oven long enough to become firm and light golden brown, about 30 minutes. Serve in slices.

Storage: These muffins will keep for about 1 week in the refrigerator.

❄ **X2** ✝⅄

HAM-ON-RYE MUFFIN MEAL

Makes 6 muffin-size loaves

8 ounces boiled ham, cut into chunks
1½ slices rye bread, crusts removed, torn into pieces
2 tablespoons fresh parsley leaves
2 tablespoons minced scallion greens
1 egg yolk
1 tablespoon unsweetened apricot jam
1 teaspoon honey mustard (see Hint)

1. Preheat the oven to 375°F. Coat 6 cups of a standard muffin tin with nonstick baking spray.

2. Put all the ingredients except the mustard in the bowl of a food processor and process until completely ground. Spoon an equal amount of the ground mixture into each of the cups. Bake for 30 minutes.

3. Remove the muffin tin from the oven and pat the excess drippings from the tops of the muffins with a paper towel. Brush the top of each muffin with the mustard, return to the oven, and bake for 5 more minutes. Unmold and serve when cool enough to eat, or refrigerate and serve cold.

Boxed Lunch

If your little darling is going through a picky-eating stage and he doesn't seem to eat much at mealtimes, buy him his very own lunch box (let him pick it out), and fill it with tiny containers with lids. Fill each of the containers with healthful food—raisins, fruit chunks, corn puffs, peas, grated carrots, hard-boiled egg circles, cubes of cheese—and let him open his box to discover all the goodies inside.

Hint: You can use any brand of honey mustard for the glaze—there are several on the market. If you like, make your own by mixing equal quantities of honey and your favorite mustard.

Variations: If you're making this for a very young baby, or for a child who doesn't like strong flavors (Simon falls into this category), then you might like to omit the glaze.

You can also bake the mixture in a 9 x 5-inch loaf pan, leaving it in the oven long enough to become firm and light golden brown, about 30 to 40 minutes. Serve in slices.

Storage: These muffins will keep up to 1 week in the refrigerator.

❄️ **X2** 🚶

CORN AND SCALLOPS MUFFIN MEAL

Makes 6 muffin-size loaves

It's often difficult to get children to eat any fish other than canned tuna, but this combination of sweet corn, cheese, and scallops has many of the flavors that kids love.

1 tablespoon unsalted butter
1 tablespoon minced scallions (white part only)
1 tablespoon all-purpose flour
1 cup milk
¼ pound bay or sea scallops, diced
¾ cup frozen corn kernels, thawed
¼ teaspoon salt
1 egg, beaten
¼ cup (about 1 ounce) grated Swiss cheese

Family Planning

To involve your kids in meal planning, organize some family tastings so everyone can participate in making decisions about what to eat. For example, make three different salad dressings (an oil-and-vinegar type, one made with buttermilk, and a cheese-based dressing) and sit everyone around the table with some raw vegetables for dipping.

You can also bring home three different brands of ketchup—or mayonnaise, or tuna, or peanut butter—and hold a "blind" tasting (remove the foods from their original containers so no one knows which brand they are tasting), and take a vote on what the "house" brand will be.

1. Preheat the oven to 375°F. Coat 6 cups of a standard muffin tin with nonstick baking spray.

2. In a medium saucepan over medium heat, melt the butter and sauté the scallions for 1 minute. Whisk in the flour and cook for 1 minute, then whisk in the milk. Cook, stirring constantly, for 3 to 4 minutes, or until thickened and bubbling.

3. Remove from heat and stir in the scallops, corn, salt, and egg. Spoon an equal amount of the mixture into each of the cups. Top each muffin with an equal amount of the cheese.

4. Bake for 30 minutes, or until the cheese is flecked with brown and the custard is firm. Unmold and serve when cool enough to eat, or refrigerate and serve cold.

Variations: This recipe can be prepared with any other fresh fish fillets, such as flounder, sole, or scrod, that you have diced into small pieces.

You can also bake the mixture in a 1-quart casserole, leaving it in the oven long enough to become firm and light golden brown, about 30 to 40 minutes.

Storage: These muffins will keep for about 1 week in the refrigerator.

❄ **X2** ⫟

Riverdale Public Library District

SWEET POTATO CUSTARD MUFFIN MEAL

Makes 5 custard-muffins

This recipe comes from one of my favorite food memoirs, Spoonbread and Strawberry Wine, *written by my friend Norma Jean Darden and her sister Carole. The authors recommend it as an accompaniment to ham or pork, but Simon eats it for breakfast. I've adapted it to be made in a muffin tin, for toddlers and children of all ages. The first time Simon had one he said, "M-m-m-m GOOD!"*

½ cup mashed sweet potatoes (about ½ medium potato; see Hint)
1 small ripe banana
½ cup milk
1 tablespoon granulated brown sugar
¼ teaspoon salt
1 egg yolk
2 tablespoons raisins or currants

Breakfast on the Run

Some days Simon isn't interested in breakfast, and I worry because I don't want to send him to school on an empty stomach, so I've started making a creamy milk-shake that I adapted from an old book of Dr. Lendon Smith's: ¾ cup milk, 6 cubes frozen milk (frozen in an ice cube tray), ½ frozen banana (peeled before freezing), ¼ cup peanut butter, and 1 tablespoon honey. I mix these ingredients in a blender until smooth and creamy, and serve the shake to him in a tall paper cup with a straw, so he can drink it on the way to school.

Hole in One

As children, my brothers and I loved something we called "Hole in One." It's made by cutting out a small circle from the center of a piece of bread, using the rim of a glass, and putting the bread into a frying pan with melted butter. Break an egg into the hole and cook it on both sides until golden brown.

1. Preheat the oven to 300°F. Coat 5 cups of a standard muffin tin with nonstick baking spray.

2. Put all ingredients except the raisins in the bowl of a food processor and process until pureed. Stir in the raisins, then spoon an equal amount of the mixture into each of the cups.

3. Bake for 45 minutes. Unmold and serve when cool enough to eat, or refrigerate and serve cold.

Hint: You can cook a sweet potato by baking it or boiling it in the skin, just like a white potato. When it's cool enough to handle, peel off the skin with a paring knife and put the cooked potato through a ricer. You can also mash it by hand or in a food mill.

Variations: Instead of sweet potato, you can use mashed winter squash (acorn or butternut). Or you can use frozen pureed winter squash, which is packed without any additives. To make the recipe even easier, use canned mashed pumpkin, which is packed without sugar or other additives.

If you'd like to decorate these muffins, cut another banana into thin rounds and put a banana slice on top of each muffin, before or after baking.

You can also bake the mixture in a 1-quart casserole dish, leaving it in the oven long enough to become firm, about 45 minutes.

Storage: These muffins will keep for about 1 week in the refrigerator.

X2 ⫟

CHICKEN-BROCCOLI MUFFIN MEAL

Makes 6 muffin-size loaves

These are so delicious that they passed the ultimate taste test: Simon had two of them the first time I made them. The recipe is a great way to use up nutritious broccoli stems that are usually thrown away.

The muffins were inspired by a recipe in 365 Ways to Cook Chicken *by Cheryl Sedaker.*

4 ounces boneless and skinless chicken breast (about ½ chicken breast)

½ cup chopped broccoli stems (save florets for another use, such as the Almost-Chinese Broccoli, page 141)

½ cup (2 ounces) grated Swiss cheese

¼ cup chopped onion

1 tablespoon chopped fresh parsley

¾ cup evaporated milk (½ of a 12-ounce can)

2 eggs

1 teaspoon salt

½ teaspoon ground pepper

Independent Snacking

Designate a shelf in the refrigerator (or a section of a shelf) exclusively for the use of your child, to hold foods that are chosen just for him and can be eaten for snacks. Ideally, this should be a low shelf so your child can reach it without help from you. The one in our house holds a plastic canteen

Muffin Meals

(the kind with its own straw) filled with cold water, and usually some foods such as raisins in tiny boxes, hard-boiled eggs, cubes of cheese, grapes, miniature rice crackers, and celery sticks—and seasonal things like strawberries and cherries. All the fruits and vegetables are washed and cut up, so that Simon is quite autonomous at snack time.

1. In enough water to cover, poach the chicken over medium-high heat for 15 minutes, or until cooked through.

2. Preheat the oven to 400°F. Coat 6 cups of a standard muffin tin with nonstick baking spray.

3. Put all the ingredients, including the cooked chicken, in the bowl of a food processor and process until pureed. Spoon an equal amount of the chicken mixture into each of the cups. Bake for 40 minutes, or until firm to the touch and light golden brown. Unmold and serve when cool enough to eat, or refrigerate and serve cold.

Variations: You can use leftover cooked chicken for this; for that matter, you can use any cooked meat or fish instead of the chicken—even canned tuna. The equivalent for any cooked meat or fish is ½ cup.

You can also bake the mixture in a 9 x 5-inch loaf pan, leaving it in the oven long enough to become firm and light golden brown, about 45 minutes. Serve in slices.

Storage: These muffins will keep for about 1 week in the refrigerator.

❄ **X2** ⚤

SPINACH SOUFFLÉ MUFFIN MEAL

Makes 12 muffins

I found this recipe at the Pillsbury Bake-Off in Phoenix in February 1990. It was submitted by Marietta Kilgore, from Beaverton, Oregon. Simon ate three muffins for breakfast the first time I made them. We've since had them at lunch and dinner, too.

1½ cups self-rising flour *or* 1½ cups all-purpose flour plus 2 teaspoons baking powder and ¾ teaspoon salt

¾ cup yellow cornmeal

1 (10-ounce) package frozen chopped spinach, thawed and squeezed dry

1 cup (4 ounces) grated cheddar cheese

⅔ cup buttermilk (see Hint)

¼ cup vegetable oil

4 eggs, separated

¼ cup sugar

Miracle Muffins

Here's a remarkably easy recipe for miniature muffins that are fun to make with and for kids: Mix 1 cup self-rising flour and 1 cup softened vanilla ice cream (I use a super-premium brand such as Häagen-Dazs). Coat the cups of a small muffin tin with nonstick baking spray and fill them three-fourths full with the batter; bake at 350°F.

for 20 minutes. They're not too sweet, so grown-ups like them, too. I've made these muffins with chocolate ice cream, peanut butter ice cream, and raspberry ice cream, and they're just as delicious.

(Note: If you don't have self-rising flour, you can substitute 1 cup all-purpose flour, 1½ teaspoons baking powder, and ½ teaspoon salt.)

1. Preheat the oven to 375°F. Coat 12 cups of a standard muffin tin with nonstick baking spray.

2. Put the flour, cornmeal, spinach, cheese, buttermilk, oil, and egg yolks in the bowl of a mixer. Blend until ingredients are completely mixed.

3. Whip the egg whites until soft peaks form. Gradually add the sugar, beating until stiff peaks form. Fold the beaten whites into the spinach mixture.

4. Spoon the batter evenly into the muffin cups (cups will be very full). Bake for 17 to 20 minutes, or until a toothpick inserted in the center comes out clean. Cool 1 minute, then remove from pan. Serve warm or at room temperature.

Hint: Instead of buttermilk, you can substitute 2 teaspoons vinegar or lemon juice mixed into ⅔ cup milk. Let stand 5 minutes before adding to batter.

Storage: These muffins will keep in the refrigerator for 3 days.

PASTA AND PIZZA

I spend a lot of my working time traveling around the world, and wherever I go I ask mothers to tell me about how they feed their children. It interests me to find that their frustrations and successes seem to be the same, regardless of the continent. The one food that kids in every country love to eat is pasta, in all its sundry forms: *nouilles, nudeln, tallarin, udon,* spaghetti, noodles, macaroni and cheese, casseroles, and canned (as in Spaghetti-Os). And, of course, there's always pizza. A friend of mine commented that it should be its own basic food group, since it's so beloved *and* helps build strong bodies. In this chapter I have come up with some variations on these tried-and-true favorites.

The Littlest Gourmet

Sara Moulton, chef of the executive dining room of *Gourmet* magazine, told me that one of her four-year-old daughter's favorite dishes is alphabet noodles tossed with olive oil and salt and pepper. Another food she likes is a breakfast called "Banana and Orange Juice Soup," which is nothing more than fresh orange juice poured into a bowl with sliced bananas floating in it.

DONNA DOHERTY'S LENTILS AND PASTA

Makes about 6 cups

This dish was created by Donna Doherty, wife of executive chef John Doherty of the Waldorf-Astoria Hotel in New York City. It can serve as a main course or as a side dish.

¾ cup lentils
1 tablespoon olive oil
1 teaspoon minced garlic
1 (8-ounce) can tomato sauce
1¾ cups water
1 chicken bouillon cube
2 cups ditalini pasta
Salt
¼ cup grated Parmesan or Locatelli cheese

1. Cover the lentils with water and soak them overnight at room temperature.

2. Heat the olive oil in a 2-quart pot over medium heat. Add the garlic and sauté for 1 minute. Add the tomato sauce, drained lentils, water, and bouillon cube. Cover pot and bring to a boil, reduce heat to simmer, and cook until lentils are tender, 20 to 30 minutes.

3. Cook the pasta in a large amount of boiling salted water, drain, and mix with the cooked lentils and cheese.

Storage: This will keep well in the refrigerator for 4 days.

🔲 ❄️ **X2** 🚶

KASHA AND BOW TIES

Makes 2 cups

Since babies and children love pasta in all forms, one day I decided to make this for Simon, to see if it would appeal to him. It's a traditional Russian-Jewish dish, and it fits right into the "nouvelle grandma" cooking that's in vogue right now. Simon doesn't know any of that; he just loves the taste.

¼ cup kasha (see Hint)
1 egg, beaten
⅓ cup minced onion
1 tablespoon unsalted butter *or* olive oil
½ cup boiling water
¼ teaspoon salt
⅔ cup (2 ounces) small egg bow tie pasta

Pasta with Mashed Potato Sauce

Barry and Susan Wine, owners of the four-star Quilted Giraffe restaurant in New York City, have two grown children. One of their favorite dishes is "Pasta with Mashed Potato Sauce and Plum Tomatoes."

The dish is prepared by making mashed potatoes, adding butter and half-and-half during the mashing process to make a smooth mixture; then milk and half-and-half are added again, in equal proportions, to thin the potatoes to a thick souplike consistency. Season with salt and pepper and pour over cooked rotelle or fusilli pasta.

Season chopped plum tomatoes (either fresh or canned) with fresh thyme, minced shallots, salt, and pepper and gently warm. Add a dash of balsamic vinegar, then spoon the just-warm tomato mixture onto the pasta.

1. In a heavy, small saucepan over very low heat, combine kasha with egg. Stir frequently until each grain is separate and dry, about 3 minutes. Remove from heat and set aside for a moment.

2. In a small skillet, sauté the onion in the butter or olive oil for 3 to 4 minutes, until onion is soft but not brown.

3. Put the sautéed onion, boiling water, and salt into the saucepan with the kasha. Stir to combine, cover, and cook over medium heat for 10 minutes, or until all liquid has evaporated; stir occasionally.

4. In the meantime, cook the pasta in 1 quart of lightly salted boiling water for 10 to 12 minutes, or until tender. Drain and stir into kasha mixture. Serve when cool enough to eat.

Hint: Kasha is a coarse brown grain that is also known as buckwheat groats. It's sold in the supermarket in a small box, usually near the rice section.

Storage: This dish will keep for up to 3 days in the refrigerator.

🖬 ❄ **X2** 🚶 🛒

HELEN CHARDACK'S BROAD NOODLE LASAGNA WITH PUREED SWEET POTATO AND RICOTTA

Makes about 4 cups

Helen Chardack, who created this recipe, is a professional chef (a graduate of the Culinary Institute of America) and the wife of Alfred Portale, chef of the three-star Gotham Bar & Grill in New York City. They are the parents of three-year-old Olympia.

¼ pound lasagna noodles (about 5 noodles)
1 cup mashed sweet potato (about 1 medium potato; see Hint)
½ cup ricotta cheese
1 egg
1 teaspoon minced fresh parsley
¾ teaspoon salt

1. Cook the lasagna noodles according to package directions until soft; drain, reserving ¼ cup of the cooking water.

2. Preheat the oven to 350°F.

Oh Boy–Orzo!

Orzo is rice-shaped pasta, and it is found in the pasta section of the supermarket. It takes only 8 to 10 minutes to cook. When Simon was a toddler, I mixed cooked orzo with grated cheese and a jar of pureed baby food that was still on the shelf from his younger months—for example, carrots or peas. Orzo has a creamy consistency that children love, and this preparation is a good way to use up jars of baby food that might otherwise go to waste. (Be sure to check the expiration date on the jars.)

Now that he's older, I cook orzo and mix it with ricotta and Parmesan cheese, and sometimes bits of leftover cooked meat and/or vegetables. It's a nice change from elbow macaroni.

3. Stir together the sweet potato, ricotta, egg, parsley, and salt; add the reserved cooking water. Cut the cooked noodles into small pieces—the size will depend on the age of your child—and stir gently into the sweet potato mixture. Put this mixture into an ovenproof dish just large enough to hold it (approximately 1 quart capacity) and bake for 30 minutes. Serve warm or at room temperature. (If you are making this for an older child, you might like to layer the whole cooked noodles and sweet potato mixture as for a lasagna.)

Hints: You can cook a sweet potato by microwaving it, baking it, or boiling it in the skin, just like a white potato. When it's cool enough to handle, peel off the skin with a paring knife and put the cooked potato through a ricer or a wire mesh sieve. You can also mash it by hand.

I like to use whole wheat lasagna noodles, and I cook them for 11 minutes before adding to the sweet potato mixture.

Variation: To make the recipe even easier, use canned mashed pumpkin, which is packed without any sugar or other additives.

Cooking ahead of time: You can make up the lasagna and refrigerate it for a day before cooking. Bake it just before mealtime, adding 5 minutes to the baking time if it's just been taken out of the refrigerator.

Storage: This will keep in the refrigerator for 3 days.

❄ **X2** ⚲ ⚲

SUMMER PASTA WITH NO-COOK SAUCE

Makes 2 cups

This was first made for us by Luciano Pavarotti—who is almost as good a cook as he is a tenor—at a party in our apartment in New York several years ago. It's a simple recipe that he likes to prepare in hotel rooms, when he's singing in different cities around the world. The sauce is so creamy that you can't imagine it hasn't been cooked.

This is best made in the summer, when you can get fresh, ripe tomatoes. It takes just a few minutes to prepare, but it is so addictively delicious that everybody in the family will want a bowl.

1 large ripe tomato, peeled, seeded, and cut into ½-inch
      cubes (see Hints)
¼ cup olive oil (see Hints)
¼ cup basil *or* flat parsley leaves, shredded
1 garlic clove, cut in half
½ teaspoon salt
Freshly ground pepper to taste
¼ pound (4 ounces) pasta (see Hints)

1. In a large serving bowl, mix the tomato cubes, olive oil, basil or parsley, garlic, salt, and pepper.

2. Cook the pasta in a large amount of salted water. While it's draining, remove the garlic from the sauce and discard. Mix the pasta into the bowl with the sauce and toss. Serve hot, or at room temperature (see Hints).

Perfect Pasta for Children

Piero Selvaggio, owner of the acclaimed Valentino and Primi restaurants in Los Angeles, has two little boys who live on pasta. Every day the family sits down for dinner together at 5:00 P.M., so Piero can go to work in his restaurants in the evening. The boys often eat rotelle, a corkscrew-shaped pasta, with tomato sauce, sausages, and garlic. Piero experimented with many different shapes of pasta before settling on rotelle, because it's easy to eat with a fork as well as to pick up with small hands.

Hints: Tomatoes are easily peeled by dropping them in a pot of boiling water, waiting for about 30 seconds, then removing them. The skins will slip off with the aid of a sharp paring knife. (This also works for peaches, by the way.)

Be sure to choose an olive oil that has a strong, assertive olive taste. It doesn't need to be an expensive extra-virgin variety, however; Goya is a supermarket brand that has good flavor.

Use any long, thin pasta shape that you like; I usually use whole wheat spaghetti or spaghettini.

When Simon was 2 years old, he insisted on eating with a fork or a spoon, which made getting slippery strands of spaghetti into his mouth a bit tricky, if not dangerous. At that stage, we chopped the cooked spaghetti into tiny pieces that he could scoop up with a spoon.

Note: This dish can be served hot, just when it's made, or at room temperature—which means you can make it up ahead of time, if you like. If you refrigerate it, you will probably want to bring it to room temperature before serving it.

Cooking ahead of time: You can prepare the pasta sauce ahead of time, up to 24 hours before serving. At mealtime, finish the recipe by completing step 2.

Storage: This pasta will last for 2 days in the refrigerator; be sure to bring it to room temperature before serving it.

30 **X2** 👫

PEANUT BUTTER NOODLES

Makes 2 cups

This is a version of the sesame noodle dish that is so popular in American Chinese restaurants.

1 cup pasta (see Hints)
¼ cup creamy peanut butter
¼ cup chicken broth
2 teaspoons freeze-dried chives
2 teaspoons reduced-sodium soy sauce
2 teaspoons rice vinegar (see Hints)
1 teaspoon honey
1 teaspoon grated fresh ginger
1 tablespoon sesame seeds

1. Cook the pasta according to the package directions and drain.

2. While the pasta is cooking, combine the peanut butter, broth, chives, soy sauce, rice vinegar, honey, and ginger in the bowl of a food processor or blender. Process until smooth.

3. Pour sauce over the drained noodles and toss well. Sprinkle the sesame seeds over noodles and serve warm, cold, or at room temperature.

Peanut Butter, But . . .

Instead of jelly, pair peanut butter with one of the following: apple butter, raisins, shredded carrots, molasses, sliced apple, alfalfa sprouts, chopped dried fruit, sliced banana, or crumbled bacon. If your child is given peanut butter in one or more of these combinations from the time he is tiny, then he will probably prefer it that way (I recommend organic).

And how about sesame butter, instead of peanut butter? You can find it in health food stores, and sometimes in the ethnic section of supermarkets under the name *tahini*. Sesame is an extremely good source of calcium. If you are worried that your child isn't getting enough calcium (if he turns up his nose at milk and yogurt, for example), then you can mix sesame butter and peanut butter and spread it on sandwiches.

A safety note: Always serve peanut butter on a cracker, piece of fruit, or other food that requires chewing. Never give a child peanut butter from a spoon; the peanut butter can become lodged in his throat and cause choking.

Hints: You can use any kind of pasta for this recipe—spaghetti or spaghettini, macaroni, flat egg noodles, spirals, radiatori, egg bow ties. I like to use short pastas when I cook for Simon, because they're easy to pick up with a spoon, fork, or fingers. Three-color pastas (the green ones are colored with spinach and the red ones with tomato) are fun for kids to eat.

Freeze-dried chives and sesame seeds are available in the spice section of the supermarket.

Rice vinegar, which has a gentle flavor and is slightly sweet, is available in the supermarket ethnic-foods section. You can also buy the product called sushi vinegar, which is sold under the Sushi Chef label of the Baycliff Company. I like to use brown rice vinegar, which I buy at health food stores.

Cooking ahead of time: You can make the sauce (step 2) and refrigerate it for up to 4 days; you might even like to make a large batch to have on hand for several meals. Then, just before serving, cook the pasta and toss with the amount of sauce you need.

Storage: These noodles will keep for 1 week in the refrigerator.

🖫 **X2** 🚶

LO MEIN

Makes 6 to 8 servings

This is another of Madge Rosenberg's favorite recipes from the days when she taught children how to cook.

1½ tablespoons cornstarch
2 tablespoons reduced-sodium soy sauce
2 tablespoons dry sherry
1 pound egg noodles
5½ tablespoons vegetable oil
1 teaspoon salt
1 teaspoon minced fresh ginger
2 garlic cloves, minced
6 cups peeled, shredded vegetables, such as broccoli,
     kohlrabi, bok choy, leeks, water chestnuts, snowpeas,
     bean sprouts, carrots, mushrooms
1 teaspoon sugar
1 cup chicken broth
2 cups shredded cooked pork, beef, poultry, or fish

Macaroni and Cheese—But for Real

In our house, this dish, a classic favorite, does not come out of a box, nor is it a big production. I boil whole wheat elbow macaroni for five minutes, then add a handful of frozen vegetables. After 10 minutes of total cooking time, when the macaroni is done, I drain off the water, then stir in some grated cheese.

As Simon grew older, he began to pick out the vegetables, so I devised a way to disguise them beyond recognition: Make a white sauce by melting 2 tablespoons of butter (or oil) in a small saucepan and then stirring in 2 tablespoons of flour to make a paste. Stir in 1 cup of milk, bring to a boil, stirring, then put in ¾ cup frozen vegetables; simmer and stir over medium heat for about 10 minutes. Add 1 cup of grated cheddar cheese, and salt and pepper; stir the sauce over low heat until the cheese has melted. Put into a blender or food processor and process until it's completely smooth. Pour it over 3 cups of cooked macaroni. To freeze (and later microwave) for future meals, cool and spoon into individual containers.

1. In a small bowl, stir together the cornstarch, soy sauce, and sherry and set aside. Bring a large pot of water to a boil. Cook the noodles until done; drain and rinse in a colander and set aside.

2. Heat 3 tablespoons of the oil in a wok or a very large skillet and add the noodles. Add the salt and stir-fry for about 3 minutes. Transfer to a serving dish and keep warm.

3. In the same wok (without washing), heat the remaining 2½ tablespoons of the oil and add the ginger, garlic, and harder vegetables (kohlrabi, broccoli, carrots). Stir-fry for 3 minutes. Add the softer vegetables (mushrooms, leeks, and so on) and stir-fry for 1 more minute. Add the sugar and stir. Add bean sprouts and stir-fry for a few seconds. Add the broth and bring to a boil, then stir in the cornstarch mixture. Add the meat or fish and stir until the sauce has thickened. Mix the vegetables and meat with the noodles and serve immediately.

Cooking ahead of time: You can prepare all of the ingredients up to 24 hours ahead of time and refrigerate them. Then, just before serving, finish the recipe, beginning with step 2.

Storage: This dish will keep in the refrigerator for 2 days.

BRADLEY OGDEN'S BREAKFAST PIZZA

Makes 4 individual pizzas

Bradley Ogden, the chef-owner of the Larkspur Inn in northern California, is famous for his opulent breakfasts, which I first sampled when he was the chef of the Campton Place Hotel in San Francisco. He came up with the following fantasy breakfast for his own three children.

DOUGH

2 cups all-purpose flour

2 tablespoons baking powder

½ teaspoon coarse salt

4 tablespoons (½ stick) cold unsalted butter, cut into 6
    pieces

½ cup milk

1 egg, lightly beaten

2 tablespoons olive oil

TOPPING

4 strips bacon, diced

½ cup diced onion

⅓ cup diced green bell pepper

2 small red new potatoes, boiled and diced

Coarse salt to taste

Freshly ground black pepper to taste

1 ripe medium tomato

1 tablespoon olive oil

1 cup grated cheese (such as Monterey Jack or American)

½ teaspoon dried oregano

4 eggs

2 tablespoons chopped fresh parsley

Mom, Can I Have Pizza for Breakfast?

When Simon was two years old, he and I were on a vacation together, and he woke up one morning groggy with jet lag, demanding a pizza for breakfast. I rummaged around in an unfamiliar kitchen and found some English muffins and other appropriate fixings and created the following recipe: Split the muffins and spread each half with a little ketchup. Sprinkle grated Parmesan on top of the ketchup, then spoon scrambled eggs on top of the cheese. The heat from the eggs will melt the cheese.

Baby Boomer Breakfast

As a child, I probably ate one dish more than any other. But just in case this simple nursery food passed your household by: Soft-boil an egg, remove the yolk and white from the shell with a spoon, and put into a bowl. Tear a slice of toast (buttered or not, as you like) into tiny pieces. Put the toast pieces into the bowl with the egg along with a little salt, mix, and lightly mash everything together. Your child can assist by tearing the toast—it was always *my* favorite part.

1. *To prepare the dough:* Put the flour, baking powder, and salt into the bowl of a food processor. Add the butter and process until the mixture has a cornmeallike texture. Add the milk and egg and process just until a dough is formed. Turn dough out onto a floured board and divide into 4 equal pieces. Pat each piece out on a baking sheet to form a 6-inch circle. Brush the circles with the 2 tablespoons olive oil.

2. Preheat the oven to 450°F.

3. *To prepare the topping:* Place the bacon in a medium skillet over medium heat. Cook, stirring occasionally, until the bacon is lightly browned. Add the onion and green pepper and cook for 5 minutes, stirring once or twice. Add the potatoes, season with salt and pepper, and cook for 3 more minutes. Remove from the heat and cool.

4. Cut the tomato into very thin slices. Lay out the slices on a plate and season with salt, pepper, and the olive oil.

5. To assemble the pizzas, distribute the tomato slices evenly among the dough circles. Top each with even amounts of the potato mixture, grated cheese, and oregano. Bake for 10 minutes, or until the cheese has melted. Remove from the oven and break 1 egg onto the top of each pizza. Sprinkle with salt and pepper and return to the oven to bake until the whites of the eggs have set and the yolks are cooked to your liking (runny or hard). Sprinkle with chopped parsley and serve.

Cooking ahead of time: You can prepare the potato topping (step 3) the night before serving the pizzas.

❄ **X2** ✝👤

RICOTTA MINI-PIZZAS

Makes ten to twelve 3-inch pizzas or
one 9½ x 12-inch pizza

I had a hard time deciding whether or not to put home-made pizza into this book. On the one hand, it might be the food most loved by American children, but who wants to spend hours making pizza dough?

Then I discovered a new product—Pillsbury All-Ready Pizza Crust—in the dairy case of my supermarket. It comes in one of those tubes that you smack against the edge of the counter to open—a participatory plus for older children.

The dough is a cinch to use, and it makes a delicious crust. Best of all, you can choose which kinds of—health-ful—toppings you like, and if you want only a child-size portion of pizza, you don't have to leave the house to get a slice.

1 (10-ounce) tube Pillsbury All-Ready Pizza Crust
¼ cup tomato sauce, homemade or from a can or jar
¼ cup minced vegetables, such as red or green bell pepper, zucchini, cauliflower, broccoli (optional; see Variations)
¼ cup ricotta cheese

Mouseketeer's Pizza

Wolfgang Puck, chef-owner of the celebrated Spago and Chinois-on-Main restaurants in Los Angeles (among others), made New Wave pizza famous in America, and lucky children who eat in Spago with their movie star parents get to eat the restaurant's Mickey Mouse pizza. Wolf bakes two small pizzas and cuts one in half to make two half-circles, which become Mickey's ears on the top of the first pizza. Mickey's eyes and nose are made of olives and a shiitake mushroom, and his mouth is made of a tomato.

1. Preheat the oven to 475°F.

2. Using your hands, pat out the pizza dough to ¼ inch thickness (or to ⅛ inch thickness if you prefer a thinner crust). With a biscuit cutter or the rim of a glass, cut out circles that are approximately 3 inches in diameter. Press the trimmings together and cut out as many circles as you can. Place the rounds about 1 inch apart on a cookie sheet coated with nonstick baking spray.

3. Spread 1 teaspoon of the tomato sauce on each dough circle. Top with some chopped vegetables, if you like, and then drop 1 teaspoon of ricotta on top (neatness doesn't count). Bake for 10 to 13 minutes, or until the crust is puffed and brown.

Variations: Sometimes I make these pizzas with very thin slices of peeled eggplant topped with the cheese.

Use other kinds of cheese, such as Parmesan, mozzarella, Monterey Jack, or cheddar, in combination with or instead of the ricotta.

Look for other brands of pizza dough in your supermarket; sometimes they are sold in the refrigerated section near the milk products, and sometimes in the freezer case.

Storage: Once cooked, these pizzas will last for about 4 days in the refrigerator. Reheat in the microwave or in a low oven.

X2

CAROL TIHANY'S MOTHER'S REVENGE

Makes approximately 8 cups

Carol got this recipe from her mother, Bess Godley Lyon (who called it something else, I think). It's an ingenious and delicious way to use up leftover macaroni and cheese, which Carol says can be a problem in some households.

¾ pound ground beef
2 tablespoons minced onion
1 (14-ounce) can tomato wedges
1 envelope instant low-sodium beef broth
4 cups leftover macaroni and cheese, in bite-size pieces

1. Preheat oven to 350°F.

2. Cook the ground beef over medium heat until lightly browned, then drain off the fat. Place the meat along with the minced onion in a casserole.

3. Drain the juice from the tomato wedges into a measuring cup and add water (if necessary) to make ¾ cup liquid. Add the envelope of beef broth and stir.

4. Put the macaroni and the tomato wedges in the casserole and pour the liquid over them. Stir ingredients until well mixed.

5. Bake for 20 minutes, or until bubbly.

Storage: This casserole will keep for 2 days in the refrigerator.

CHICKEN AND TURKEY

I am willing to bet that anyone who cooks for a family is on the lookout for new ways to cook poultry: it's inexpensive, it's low in fat, and almost everyone likes it. Surprisingly, however, Simon has never been inclined to eat chicken or turkey, unless it's transformed in some way. Since I'd like him to eat plenty of low-fat protein (most of the nonmeat sources, such as dairy and eggs, have some nutritional drawbacks), I developed the following recipes to tickle his taste buds.

CRUNCHY CHICKEN DRUMSTICKS

Makes 4 drumsticks

The cereal that coats the chicken pieces here makes an incredibly crunchy crust that is irresistible. Children, I have found, love the crunchy texture more than the taste of the chicken—not unlike most grown-ups I know! Taking the skin off before marinating reduces the fat content of the chicken considerably.

2 tablespoons creamy peanut butter, at room temperature
1 cup peach juice (see Hints)
2 tablespoons reduced-sodium soy sauce
1 tablespoon grated fresh ginger (optional)
4 chicken legs, skin removed and discarded (or used in chicken stock)
1 cup Grape Nuts cereal

1. In a blender or food processor, blend the peanut butter, peach juice, soy sauce, and ginger until smooth.

2. Pour this mixture into a plastic bag and add the chicken legs. Marinate in the refrigerator for at least 1 hour or overnight, turning the bag once or twice.

3. Preheat the oven to 350°F.

4. Put the cereal into another plastic bag. Remove each piece of chicken from the marinade and put it into the bag with the cereal. Close the bag and shake to coat the chicken thoroughly.

Label Lingo

The difference between "enriched" and "fortified" on labels of packaged food is that enriched food contains more of the vitamins that naturally occur in it; fortified food contains vitamins that do not naturally occur in it.

5. Place the chicken in a baking pan coated with non-stick baking spray. Drizzle a bit of the remaining marinade over the chicken pieces. Bake for 45 minutes, or until the juices run clear when the legs are pierced. You can drizzle some of the leftover marinade over the legs once or twice during the baking time. Serve when cool enough to eat.

Hints: Peach (or apricot) juice made without additives is available in health food stores. Most supermarkets sell peach or apricot nectar in cans and bottles, which will work well, too.

Variation: Any part of the chicken will work in this recipe, as long as you take the skin off before marinating. Thighs will take about 35 to 40 minutes to cook; breasts on the bone, about 30 minutes; boneless breasts, about 20 minutes.

To prepare 1 piece of chicken, use 2 teaspoons peanut butter, $\frac{1}{4}$ cup peach juice, 2 teaspoons soy sauce, and 1 teaspoon grated fresh ginger for the marinade. Reduce the Grape Nuts to $\frac{1}{4}$ cup, and bake according to the directions.

Cooking ahead of time: You can marinate the chicken for up to 24 hours ahead of time, then continue with the recipe in step 3.

Storage: The cooked chicken will keep for about 4 days in the refrigerator.

X2 ϯ⋏

CHICKEN NUGGETS

Makes 12 pieces

2 eggs, beaten, *or* 1 egg and 2 tablespoons water, beaten
    together
1 cup cornflakes, crushed lightly with your hands
⅓ cup all-purpose flour
1 boneless and skinless chicken breast (about 6 ounces),
    cut into 1- to 2-inch chunks (pieces add up to about ¾
    cup)

1. Preheat the oven to 400°F. Coat a baking pan or cake pan with nonstick baking spray.

2. Place the beaten egg in a bowl and the crushed cornflakes in a separate bowl. Put the flour in a plastic or paper bag and add the chicken; close the bag and shake to coat the chicken with flour. Pour the chicken chunks into a mesh strainer and shake off all the excess flour over a wastebasket or a sink. One by one, dip each flour-coated chicken chunk into the egg, then into the cornflakes, making sure it is thoroughly coated with each substance. As they are coated, put the chicken chunks into the baking pan.

3. Bake for 10 to 12 minutes, or until cooked through.

Variation: If you'd like a dip for these, you can mix 1 part ketchup, 2 parts mayonnaise, and a dollop of pickle relish.

Storage: You can store these nuggets in the refrigerator for up to 2 days, and reheat them in a low oven or in a microwave.

🕒 ❄️ **X2** 🚶

A Professional Chef's Trick

If you want to add a hard-boiled egg yolk to a dish to fortify it, mince it by pressing the yolk through the holes of a metal mesh strainer. Hard-boiled egg whites mince easily on the medium-size holes of a four-sided grater.

POPEYE PATTIES

Makes about 10 tiny patties

This is a great way to feed spinach to a child who won't come within ten feet of a green vegetable. The ingredients add up to a complete meal, and the crusty texture makes these little patties irresistible.

1 boneless and skinless chicken breast (about 6 ounces), cut into 1- to 2-inch chunks (pieces add up to about ¾ cup)
½ slice whole wheat bread, torn into 4 pieces
¼ cup frozen chopped spinach, thawed
1 egg yolk
½ teaspoon salt
1 tablespoon vegetable oil

1. Put all ingredients except the vegetable oil into a food processor and process until finely ground.

2. Heat the oil in a medium skillet over medium-high heat. Drop 1 tablespoon of the mixture into the skillet for each patty and sauté until brown on one side, about 1 minute; flip patties and sauté until brown on the other side, about 1 minute. Serve when cool enough to eat.

Variations: Any other kind of meat can be used instead of chicken: beef, lamb, turkey—even pork.

Storage: When I am making these, I usually make up the raw mixture and sauté as many patties as I need at that time, leaving the remaining mixture in the refrigerator, where it keeps for up to 4 days.

CHICKEN RÖSTI

Makes one 7-inch pancake

This dish originated in Switzerland, where it is as ubiquitous as french fries are in the United States. It's like a large potato pancake, and just as crisp and delicious. My version has meat in it, to add some protein.

When Simon is at his most picky, and doesn't want to eat anything, I've been known to call this "potato pizza," which entices him to clean his plate.

1 boneless and skinless chicken breast (about 6 ounces),
    cooked and diced (about ½ cup cooked meat)
1 medium baking potato, peeled and grated
1 tablespoon all-purpose flour
1 egg, lightly beaten
1 tablespoon minced onion
Salt and freshly ground pepper to taste
2 tablespoons vegetable oil

1. In a small bowl, mix all of the ingredients except the oil.

2. Coat a small, heavy skillet (preferably nonstick) with nonstick baking spray. Heat 1 tablespoon of the oil in the skillet over medium heat and add the potato mixture, pressing down with the back of a wooden spoon to flatten it evenly. Cook for about 5 minutes, or until the underside is browned.

3. Push a spatula under the *rösti* to loosen it from the skillet, then turn it out onto a dinner plate by placing the plate on the top of the skillet, holding onto the skillet and plate together with 2 oven mitts, and flipping it over.

4. Pour the remaining tablespoon of oil into the skillet, heat it, and slide in the *rösti,* raw side down. Cook for 5 more minutes, or until the other side is browned.

5. Cut into wedges, and serve when cool enough to eat.

Note: To make this recipe easier, put a small wedge of peeled onion into the food processor and mince it. Add the cooked chicken breast, cut into chunks, and mince it. Remove the chopping blade and put in the grating disk, then grate the peeled potato. Then combine all the prepared ingredients in a small mixing bowl.

Variations: You can use ½ cup of any cooked meat in this recipe—ham, pork, lamb, beef. Simply dice it and add it to the mixture.

Sometimes, if I feel Simon needs some extra nutrients slipped into his diet, I add grated carrots and grated apples to the potato mixture. I've eliminated the onion, for the time being, since he seems to react to strong flavors —even the innocuous onion.

For grown-up kids: You might like to serve this with a fruit chutney.

Storage: This can be kept in the refrigerator for 2 days, and eaten cold or hot. It's perfect to take on a picnic or in a lunch box, to be eaten out of hand, or you can warm it in the microwave or in a low oven.

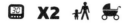

JUICY ORANGE CHICKEN

Makes 4 chicken thighs, plus vegetables

This dish is so simple to make that I can put it together at the last minute and have dinner on the table in no time. Kasha and Bow Ties is a delicious side dish for this recipe (see page 58).

4 chicken thighs
4 medium carrots, peeled and sliced into ¼-inch rounds
1 cup orange juice
2 tablespoons reduced-sodium soy sauce

1. Place the chicken thighs in a skillet or pan just large enough to hold them comfortably without crowding. Sprinkle in the sliced carrots. Pour in the orange juice and soy sauce and shake the pan a few times to distribute the liquid.

2. Bring to a boil over high heat, then lower the heat to medium-low and simmer, covered, for 20 minutes. Remove the lid and raise the heat to high; cook for 7 minutes, shaking the pan a few times to move the chicken and vegetables and prevent sticking. The sauce should be thick and syrupy. Serve when cool enough to eat.

1,001 Bites

Mark Caraluzzi, food consultant and restaurateur in Washington, D.C., told me that his five-year-old son, John, has "never been a big eater, but we can always get him to finish his meal by telling him a story while he's eating." The story is told in installments, and will continue only if the boy takes a bite of dinner.

Variations: Frozen sliced carrots can be substituted for the fresh carrots. You can also substitute fresh peeled beets, cut into ½-inch cubes, for the carrots.

You can make this in smaller quantities, if you like. Simply subtract the ingredients proportionately: 1 chicken thigh takes 1 carrot, ¼ cup orange juice, and ½ tablespoon soy sauce, and so on. Be sure to use a proportionately smaller pan and, after the 20-minute cooking time, boil the sauce over high heat for just enough time to reduce the sauce to a syrupy texture (this last step will probably take fewer than the 7 minutes allotted in the original recipe).

Storage: This dish can be refrigerated for up to 3 days and reheated in a microwave or on top of the stove over low heat.

🖳 **X2** 🚶‍♂️ 🍼

TEENY CHICKEN DUMPLINGS

Makes about 35 very small chicken balls

These baby dumplings are delicious by themselves or in a clear soup. They are also a great way to put turnips, or other strong-tasting vegetables, into a child's diet—although you can certainly substitute a more customary vegetable.

This recipe was inspired by a recipe in Elizabeth Andoh's book At Home with Japanese Cooking.

8 ounces boneless and skinless chicken breast, cut up
    (about 1½ chicken breasts)
1 egg white
1 teaspoon cornstarch
¼ teaspoon grated orange *or* lemon rind (dried or fresh)
1 teaspoon sugar
1 tablespoon reduced-sodium soy sauce
½ cup peeled and coarsely chopped turnips
1 tablespoon coarse salt

1. Grind all ingredients except salt together in a food processor.

2. Put 2 quarts of water and the salt in a medium-pot and bring to a rapid boil; reduce heat so water simmers.

3. Using a teaspoon and/or your hands, form the mixture into small balls about 1 inch in diameter, and drop them, in small batches, into the simmering water. Use a slotted spoon to gently scrape the balls off the bottom of the pot, so that they float to the top. Poach for 10 minutes, until chicken is cooked through. Drain on paper towels and serve when cool enough to eat. If you're serving them in soup, at this point you can simply transfer the dumplings to the finished soup and serve.

Variations: These dumplings can also be poached in chicken stock or broth; it will give them a richer flavor and you can use the poaching liquid later in another recipe.

Any other root vegetable—carrots, potatoes, parsnips, rutabaga—can be substituted for the turnips.

You can also sauté these as little patties in a small amount of olive oil or vegetable oil. Cook until brown and crisp on both sides.

Cooking ahead of time: You can make up the raw mixture and keep it in the refrigerator for up to 2 days, cooking the dumplings or sautéing the patties as you need them.

Storage: These cooked dumplings or patties can be refrigerated for up to 3 days.

INSTANT COUSCOUS WITH ZUCCHINI, PEAS, AND CHICKEN

Makes about 2 cups

Like many first-time mothers, Helen Chardack found that couscous is one of the easiest foods to cook and a most satisfying food to eat.

4 ounces boneless and skinless chicken breast
¼ cup frozen peas
¼ cup diced carrot
¼ cup diced yellow summer squash
¼ cup diced zucchini
Salt to taste
⅓ cup couscous
1 teaspoon minced fresh parsley
½ teaspoon raisins

Teaching Children to Love Food

Lydia Shire, the talented chef-owner of Biba restaurant in Boston, has three grown children as well as a new baby, but when asked about children's eating habits, her own childhood came to mind. She told me, "I think one of the reasons I become a chef is because of my father's specialty. On Saturday nights when I was a child, he grilled a flank steak on top of the stove over the highest heat in a flat iron griddle. He cooked it rare, and sliced it thinly on the diagonal, and served it with spaghetti tossed with olive oil and garlic. I can still taste those flavors today, when I talk about it.

"My mother also made something that taught me to love asparagus—she used to overcook it, until it was quite mushy, and served it to me on buttered toast. Most kids don't like asparagus, but I always have, even when I was small, probably because of this dish."

1. Poach the chicken over medium-high heat in enough salted water to cover for 15 to 20 minutes, or until cooked through. Remove the chicken from the water and keep warm.

2. Put the peas into the water in which you've cooked the chicken and simmer for 2 minutes. Add the carrot and simmer for 1 minute. Add the yellow squash and zucchini and simmer for 1 minute. Strain vegetables, reserving the cooking water. Put the vegetables with the chicken.

3. Measure a generous ½ cup of the cooking water and taste it for seasoning, adding salt if necessary. Bring to a boil in a small saucepan and stir in the couscous and parsley. Remove the pan from the heat, cover, and let stand for 5 minutes. Fluff with a fork and serve with the chicken, cut into bite-size pieces, and the vegetables. Moisten with extra broth, if necessary, and garnish with raisins.

Storage: This will keep in the refrigerator for 3 days, and can be reheated in the microwave or slowly over low heat, adding a little water or broth, if necessary.

X2

RICK MOONEN'S CHICKEN WITH NOODLES

Makes 2 cutlets, plus noodles and sauce (2 adult portions)

Rick Moonen is the chef of the Water Club in New York City, and the father of two sons, Geoffrey and Christopher. When I asked him for his children's favorite dish, he gave me this recipe. Rick's children like this served with corn.

1 egg and 2 tablespoons water, beaten together
¾ cup dry Italian seasoned bread crumbs
⅓ cup all-purpose flour
2 boneless and skinless chicken breasts (about 6 ounces each)
3 tablespoons olive oil
1 cup sliced mushrooms
1 can condensed cream of celery soup
1 can condensed cream of mushroom soup
1⅓ cups milk
6 ounces egg noodles (about ⅓ of a 1-pound package)

The Caterer's Apprentices

The late Leslee Reis, chef-owner of Café Provençal in Evanston, Illinois, raised two children who are in their twenties now, and she credited their good taste in food partly to the fact that she included them in her kitchen work when they were very small, when she had a catering business. She told them stories while they worked, which delighted them. She remembered teaching them from a very early age how to use a knife safely and asking them to cut up their own crudités; this "work" dovetailed nicely with their Montessori education, which stresses practical skills and respects the abilities of even the tiniest children.

1. Place the beaten egg in a bowl and the bread crumbs in a separate bowl. Put the flour in a plastic or paper bag and add the chicken cutlets; close the bag and shake to coat the chicken with flour. Shake to remove excess flour. Dip each flour-coated chicken cutlet into the egg, then into the bread crumbs, making sure they are thoroughly coated with each substance.

2. Heat the olive oil in a large skillet over medium heat and sauté the chicken for about 2 minutes on each side, or until golden brown. (The chicken won't be cooked through at this point.) Remove the chicken to a plate.

3. Sauté the mushrooms in the same pan for 3 minutes. Add the soups and the milk and bring to a boil, stirring. Replace the chicken cutlets, reduce the heat to a simmer, and cover the pan. Simmer over low heat until the chicken is cooked, about 30 minutes (check often to prevent sticking; if the sauce gets too thick during cooking, thin with a little milk or water).

4. In the meantime, cook the noodles according to package directions. When the chicken is done, serve over the cooked noodles.

For grown-up kids: Rick recommends crisp-cooked cardoon as an accompaniment.

Storage: This dish will keep in the refrigerator for 3 days.

❄ **X2** 🚶 👶

OVEN-BARBECUED CHICKEN

Makes 6 to 8 servings

This is one of those super-simple recipes that passes from housewife to housewife all across America, but Madge Rosenberg is the first to point out how good it is for kids— to make and eat!

1 package onion soup mix
1 bottle garlic-flavored French salad dressing
1 (8- to 10-ounce) jar apricot jam (no sugar added)
2 (2½- to 3-pound) chickens, each cut into 8 pieces

1. Mix the soup mix, dressing, and jam. With a brush or your hand, spread the mixture all over the chicken and marinate for at least 4 hours, but preferably overnight in the refrigerator.

2. Preheat the oven to 350°F. Bake the chicken for 45 minutes. Drain off some of the liquid and bake for an additional 15 minutes. This dish is delicious when eaten hot or cold.

Cooking ahead of time: You can marinate the chicken (step 1) for up to 24 hours ahead of time.

Storage: The cooked chicken will keep for 3 days in the refrigerator.

X2 ✝👤

GROUND TURKEY BURGERS

Makes 2 small burgers

Burgers are always easy, but these are a little more interesting than the standard. They are delicious served with Warm Eggplant Salad (page 148).

2 tablespoons milk
1 thick or 2 thin slices of bread, crusts removed and cubed
8 ounces ground turkey
2 tablespoons grated Parmesan cheese
1 teaspoon chopped fresh parsley
1 teaspoon reduced-sodium soy sauce
Salt and pepper to taste
1 teaspoon vegetable oil

1. Pour milk over bread cubes to moisten.

2. Mix the moistened bread with the turkey, cheese, parsley, soy sauce, and seasonings, and form into 2 thin burgers.

3. Sauté the burgers in the oil in a small skillet over medium heat until light brown on both sides and cooked through. Serve when cool enough to eat.

TURKEY AND VEGGIE CHILI

Makes about 1 quart

Babies and children seem to have a fondness for chili that defies logic. Because this dish is made with poultry, it has a lower fat and cholesterol content than chili made with red meat. And the (hidden) vegetables add some extra nutrients. I often serve this chili with whole wheat macaroni, corn chips, or corn or flour tortillas to make a complete meal.

1 cup diced onion

2 tablespoons vegetable oil

1 long Italian frying pepper, diced (about ¾ cup), *or* 1 red
     or green bell pepper, diced

1 large or 2 small carrots, peeled and diced (about
     ¾ cup)

1 pound ground turkey *or* chicken

1 (8-ounce) can tomato sauce *or* puree

1 cup chicken broth

2 tablespoons chili powder (see Hint)

1½ teaspoons salt

½ teaspoon ground cumin

Stop the Whining

The best piece of advice I've ever gotten about trying to limit a child's obsessive desire for sugared cereals is from a mother who told her son that he could have that sweet, brightly colored cereal he'd seen advertised on television, but he couldn't eat it for breakfast—he could only have it as a dessert after dinner.

1. In a medium saucepan, sauté the onion in the oil over medium heat for 8 minutes, stirring occasionally, until translucent.

2. Add the pepper and carrot and sauté for 2 minutes. Add the turkey or chicken and sauté for 4 minutes, stirring occasionally, until the meat loses its pink color.

3. Add the tomato sauce or puree, broth, chili powder, salt, and cumin, and bring to a boil, stirring; reduce heat so the chili simmers slowly, cover, and cook for 30 minutes, stirring occasionally. Serve when cool enough to eat.

Hint: There are 2 kinds of chili powder sold in jars in the supermarket—"hot" and plain chili powder. If you are making this for babies or children, be sure to buy the milder powder.

For grown-up kids: Grown-ups who are so inclined can add hot sauce, minced fresh hot peppers, or red pepper flakes.

If you have the extra time and energy, you can prepare some toppings to serve at the table, such as grated cheddar or Monterey Jack cheese, minced scallions, diced avocado, minced cilantro (Chinese parsley), sour cream (or yogurt), wedges of lime, and minced hot peppers.

Storage: This chili will keep in the refrigerator for up to a week, and can be reheated slowly over low heat or in the microwave.

❄ **X2** 🚶 🛒

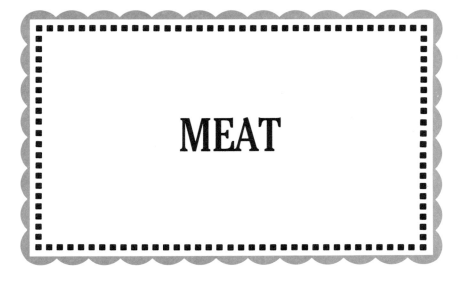

MEAT

According to Harold McGee in his book *On Food and Cooking,* we have a natural "preference for the most concentrated, most complete source of protein," which is red meat. Someone forgot to give Simon the word, however, since he is not very interested in eating plain red meat. He likes the following dishes, however, because they're not at all plain.

SOUTH-OF-THE-BORDER PICADILLO

Makes about 1½ cups

This can be served any number of ways: as a Sloppy Joe on a hamburger bun, in pita bread, with warm corn or flour tortillas, over pasta, or just plain.

8 ounces ground beef
½ cup diced onion
1 garlic clove, minced
¼ cup raisins *or* currants
1 tablespoon tomato paste
½ teaspoon salt
⅛ teaspoon ground cinnamon
⅛ teaspoon ground cumin
Freshly ground pepper to taste
2 tablespoons chopped roasted almonds *or* peanuts
    (optional)

1. In a heavy skillet over medium heat, sauté the beef, onion, and garlic together, stirring, for 8 minutes.

2. Add remaining ingredients except the nuts and lower the heat; cook, stirring, for 5 minutes. Sprinkle on the nuts and serve when cool enough to eat.

For grown-up kids: Add hot peppers or hot sauce to taste.

Storage: The cooked picadillo will last in the refrigerator for up to 4 days.

🖵 ❄ **X2** 🚶 🛒

HAMBURGERS À LA LINDSTROM

Makes 4 regular burgers or 8 small ones

This is the Swedish version of a hamburger—a meal in itself, with meat, potato, and vegetable all together. I make it with canned beets, one of the few canned products in my pantry (along with broth and tomatoes), which makes it very easy to assemble. I usually serve it plain, or sometimes with a hamburger bun; I buy small, round whole wheat rolls and split them in half horizontally to make mini hamburger buns.

8 ounces ground beef
1 medium potato, cooked, peeled, and grated (about
    ¾ cup)
1 (8¼-ounce) can cooked beets (sliced or whole), drained
    and grated (about ¾ cup)
2 eggs, lightly beaten
½ teaspoon salt
2 teaspoons vegetable oil

1. In a small bowl, mix all the ingredients except the oil. Form into patties.

2. Heat the oil in a skillet over medium heat. Cook the patties on both sides, until crusty on the outside and cooked through (time will depend on size of patties).

Variations: In Sweden, this is usually served with a fried egg on top; in Finland, it is served with mounds of golden crisp-fried onions.

For grown-up kids: You can also make this with canned pickled beets, to give the burgers a piquant flavor.

Storage: This mixture, uncooked, will keep in the refrigerator for up to 3 days. Often, I form the uncooked mixture into patties and freeze them to defrost in the microwave and pan-fry for a last-minute meal.

Yes, Sweetbreads

Sweetbreads have the same appealing texture and relative blandness as tofu, and so kids love them. Here's a recipe I devised for Simon: Cut the sweetbreads into 2-inch chunks; dip these pieces into a beaten egg, then into whole wheat bread crumbs, and sauté in olive oil for about 1 minute on each side, until the crust is golden brown.

YUMMY SAUCE FOR PASTA

Makes about 3 cups

Simon—who wouldn't pick up a meatball if his life depended on it—loves this meat sauce on spaghetti or macaroni, and doesn't know he's eating meat. Our family usually ends up sharing a bowl of pasta together, because George and I love it, too. I usually serve this with whole wheat pasta, such as spaghetti or elbow macaroni, and top with a generous amount of freshly grated cheese.

½ cup chopped carrot

½ cup chopped celery

1 small onion, chopped

1 tablespoon olive oil

½ pound ground meat (beef, pork, veal, chicken, turkey, or a combination)

1 (16-ounce) can crushed tomatoes (American brands are best)

¼ cup chopped fresh basil *or* Italian parsley leaves

½ cup chicken *or* beef broth

½ cup dry red wine

2 teaspoons coarse salt

Generous amount of freshly ground pepper

Four Hands Are Better than Two

If you are making meatballs for dinner, ask your child to participate; not only will it be fun to make dinner together but it also helps develop small motor coordination.

1. In a heavy, medium saucepan over medium heat, sauté the carrot, celery, and onion in the olive oil until the onion is transparent, about 5 minutes.

2. Add the meat and cook, stirring, for 3 to 5 minutes. Add the remaining ingredients and bring to a boil; reduce the heat to a simmer and cook, stirring occasionally, for 1 hour.

Variations: If you'd like the sauce to be smoother, puree in batches in a blender. (If you're not using it right away, let the sauce cool for at least 30 minutes before pureeing, so that it's not too difficult to handle.)

You can use this to make delicious English muffin pizzas. Spoon on some of this sauce, top with mozzarella cheese, and heat until melted and bubbly under the broiler.

Storage: This sauce will keep for about a week in the refrigerator. I usually make a double or triple batch, then freeze it in 4-ounce containers; dinner or lunch can be on the table in the amount of time it takes to cook the pasta.

❄ **X2** 🧑‍🦲 🍼

Meat

LAMB STEW WITH RAISINS

Makes about 3½ cups

I developed this simple recipe when Simon was small, about ten months old, and just beginning to eat meat. Lamb is the least allergenic of meats, and so I chose it to avoid a potential reaction. I added the raisins because I was concerned about Simon getting enough iron in his diet, and because they taste delicious with the lamb!

Since Simon is now older, I dice the cooked lamb instead of pureeing it, for a more grown-up stew.

2½ pounds lamb stewing meat on the bone, such as lamb shanks, shoulder, blade chops, riblets; *or* 2 pounds boneless lamb stewing meat, cut into large cubes
1½ cups raisins
Salt and pepper to taste

1. Place lamb and raisins in a pot large enough to hold them comfortably and cover with water. Bring to a boil over high heat, then lower the heat and simmer, covered, for 2 hours, or until the meat almost falls off the bone, or falls apart when pierced with a fork. Cool for 1 hour at room temperature, or in the refrigerator overnight.

2. If you've refrigerated the stew, remove the hardened fat from the top and discard. Put the pan over low heat to melt the cooking liquid. Pour contents of the pan into a colander placed over a bowl to catch the liquid. When cool enough to handle, remove the bones from the meat with your fingers and discard the bones. At this point, you can (depending on the age of your child) place the meat and raisins in a food processor and add enough of the cooking liquid as necessary to puree the solids, or chop the meat with the raisins and add enough of the cooking liquid to achieve the texture of a stew. Season with salt and pepper. Serve warm or at room temperature.

Note: The leftover cooking liquid can be used to cook rice, kasha, or any other grain.

Storage: This stew can be refrigerated for up to 4 days. When Simon was very small, I used to spoon it into ice cube trays, freeze the trays, and pop the cubes into a resealable plastic bag. When I needed some for a meal, I defrosted 1 or 2 cubes in the refrigerator or in a microwave.

LITTLE PORK AND POTATO TURNOVERS

Makes 8 turnovers

The filling for these turnovers is a cousin to the South-of-the-Border Picadillo (page 93). This is made with pork and potatoes; it is just as addictively delicious as the original, and it has the added nutritional benefit of niacin from the pork. The day I tested these in my kitchen, everyone in the vicinity came back again and again for more.

1 medium potato, peeled and cut into chunks
1 small or ½ medium onion, peeled and cut into chunks
1 garlic clove
8 ounces ground pork
¼ cup raisins *or* currants
2 tablespoons chopped roasted almonds *or* peanuts
1 tablespoon tomato paste
½ teaspoon salt
⅛ teaspoon ground cinnamon
⅛ teaspoon ground cumin
Freshly ground pepper to taste
2 (8-ounce) tubes Pillsbury Crescent Dinner Rolls

1. Mince the potato, onion, and the garlic in a food processor.

2. In a heavy frying pan over medium heat, sauté the potato mixture along with the pork, stirring, for 8 minutes, or until the pork is no longer pink. Add the remaining ingredients except the dough and lower the heat; cook, stirring, for 5 minutes. Cool to lukewarm or to room temperature before filling the turnovers.

3. Preheat the oven to 375°F.

4. Unroll 1 tube of the dough. Pull the dough apart at the horizontal and vertical perforations that divide it into 4 rectangles, and press together the diagonal perforations across each rectangle to seal them. Place 2 heaping tablespoons of the pork mixture in the center of each of the rectangles. Fold the dough in half over the filling and press the 3 open edges of the dough together with the tines of a fork to crimp. Repeat this process with the second tube of dough.

5. Coat a cookie sheet with nonstick baking spray, and transfer the turnovers to the sheet with a spatula. Bake 12 to 15 minutes, or until golden brown. Transfer to a rack until cool enough to eat.

Note: These can be eaten warm or at room temperature; they're perfect picnic food. If you like, you can eat the filling by itself, rather than using it to fill turnovers.

For grown-up kids: Add hot peppers or hot sauce to the filling mixture, or pass it at the table.

Cooking ahead of time: You can make the filling up to 2 days ahead and refrigerate it to fill the turnovers later.

Storage: These will keep in the refrigerator for up to 4 days. To reheat, wrap in foil and bake 8 to 10 minutes in a 350°F. oven, or until heated through.

CHICKEN LIVER CUSTARD

Makes 2 individual custards

This is a hit among those who usually can't abide liver, as well as for those who've never had it before. It's a great way to introduce liver to a child, since traditional American preparations are usually too strong tasting for children.

I learned a recipe similar to this many years ago from the great French chef Jacques Pepin. This version can be served as he recommends it, as an elegant first course or as a luncheon dish, surrounded by a flavorful tomato sauce.

⅓ cup (about 3 ounces) chicken livers (see Hint)
2 tablespoons parsley leaves
½ garlic clove
Pinch of dried thyme
1 teaspoon unsalted butter
¾ cup heavy cream *or* milk
2 eggs
½ teaspoon salt
Freshly ground pepper to taste

1. Put the chicken livers, parsley, garlic, and thyme into a food processor and process until mixture is very smooth.

2. Melt the butter in a small skillet over medium-high heat and sauté the liver mixture, stirring constantly, until liver has lost all its pink color, about 1 minute. Cool for 10 minutes.

3. Preheat the oven to 400°F. Coat two ½-cup heatproof glass or ceramic custard cups with nonstick baking spray.

This Liver He Will Like

One day, when I was making a roast chicken for dinner, I concocted this dish for Simon: Cut away the fat from the neck of the bird and melt it in a small frying pan (about 1 teaspoon of fat). Sauté 1 tablespoon of minced onion in the chicken fat for 3 or 4 minutes, then add 3 tablespoons diced potato cut into the tiniest cubes. Cook for about 5 minutes over medium-high heat, stirring until light brown. Then add the liver, minced, and sauté the dish for 3 or 4 more minutes, until the liver is cooked through. Add salt to taste.

Kiddie Hors d'Oeuvre

If you'd like your child to eat liver (it's loaded with vitamin A and the B vitamins), try to persuade him with chicken livers wrapped with bacon and broiled until crispy. Secure with a frilly toothpick, for fun.

4. Place the cooled liver mixture in a blender along with the cream or milk, eggs, salt, and pepper and blend until smooth. Pour into the prepared custard cups and place the cups in a deep baking pan (a round cake pan works well). Place the pan on the oven rack and pour enough hot water into the baking pan to come up almost to the tops of the cups. Bake, uncovered, for 40 to 45 minutes. To test doneness, pierce the center of one of the custards with a paring knife; when it comes out clean, custards are cooked. Remove cooked custards from the oven and let them sit in the hot water for 10 minutes.

5. To serve, unmold the custards onto a serving plate or cool and serve right from the custard cups.

Hint: The chicken livers can be saved and frozen from the whole chickens you buy; defrost before using.

Variations: You can make this into a chicken custard by substituting ½ cup cubed boneless and skinless chicken breast for the liver.

You can also make this in a single mold. Simply choose a small (1 cup) heatproof soufflé dish. The cooked custard can be cut into wedges and served that way.

I've made a single custard from this recipe with 1 liver, and put it in the refrigerator for a cold lunch for Simon the next day. To make 1 custard, cut the recipe in half.

Storage: You can refrigerate the custard for up to 3 days and serve it cold, or heat the cups in the microwave or in a hot water bath in a low oven.

SEAFOOD

I am convinced that fish and seafood are the last foods that most American children learn to love, maybe because they often have such strong flavors. On the other hand, fish is a nutritious, low-fat form of protein—remember when we used to call it "brain food"? Because I am not interested in disguising fish by coating it with breading and frying it beyond recognition (like the fried clams at Howard Johnson's), I conceived the following recipes for Simon—and for his parents, too.

INSTANT COUSCOUS WITH SHRIMP AND CORN

Makes 3 cups

Couscous is a form of grain made from wheat. You can find it in most supermarkets, usually in the rice section. Whole wheat couscous is sold in bulk in my health food store; it can be cooked in just the same way as the couscous you buy in a box.

1½ cups chicken broth
1 cup couscous
3 tablespoons unsalted butter *or* olive oil
¼ cup minced onion
½ cup frozen tiny shrimp, thawed
½ cup frozen corn, thawed
½ teaspoon salt

1. Bring the broth to a boil in a small saucepan. Stir in the couscous; remove from heat and cover; let stand 5 minutes. Stir lightly with a fork to fluff.

2. In a small skillet over medium heat, sauté the onion, shrimp, and corn in the butter for 5 minutes.

3. Add the shrimp mixture and salt to the couscous and toss to combine. Serve when cool enough to eat.

Variations: Instead of shrimp, use any kind of cooked or raw meat or fish, cut into tiny pieces. Instead of corn, use frozen peas.

Storage: This will keep in the refrigerator for 3 days.

X2

LITTLE FISH TURNOVERS

Makes 8 turnovers

The filling in these pies is a delicious hash, modeled after traditional recipes from New England. I've used converted rice here because it has more vitamins and nutrients than ordinary white rice.

½ cup chopped mushrooms
½ cup chopped celery
½ cup chopped carrot
¼ cup chopped onion
2 strips bacon, diced
¼ cup converted rice
2 whole tomatoes from a can, crushed with your hands
1¼ cups water
½ teaspoon dried tarragon
½ teaspoon salt
Freshly ground pepper to taste
1 fillet of sole (about 4 ounces)
2 (8-ounce) tubes Pillsbury Crescent Dinner Rolls

1. Finely chop the mushrooms, celery, carrot, and onion together in a food processor.

2. Sauté the bacon in a heavy skillet for about 3 minutes, or until crisp. With a slotted spoon, transfer the bacon to a paper towel and leave the drippings in the skillet.

3. Add the rice to the skillet and sauté over low heat for 2 minutes. Add the ground vegetables, tomatoes, ½ cup of the water, tarragon, salt, and pepper; stir. Bring to a boil, then reduce heat to low; cover and simmer for 15 minutes, or until all the liquid is absorbed (do not stir).

4. Remove the cover and stir in ¾ cup more water. Place the fish fillet on top of the mixture and sprinkle with the bacon. Cover and cook over low heat for 7 to 10 minutes, or until the fish is opaque and liquid is evaporated. (Again, do not stir.) If you are using this as a filling for pastry, mash it a bit with a fork to blend all the ingredients. If you're eating it without the pastry, serve it as is. Cool to room temperature before filling the turnovers.

5. Preheat the oven to 375°F.

6. Unroll 1 tube of the dough. Pull the dough apart at the horizontal and vertical perforations that divide it into 4 rectangles, and press together the diagonal perforations across each rectangle to seal them. Place 2 heaping table-spoons of the fish mixture in the center of each of the rectangles. Fold the dough in half over the filling and press the 3 open edges of the dough together with the tines of a fork to crimp. Repeat this process with the second tube.

7. Coat a cookie sheet with nonstick baking spray, and transfer the pastries to the sheet with a spatula. Bake 12 to 15 minutes or until golden brown. Transfer the cooked pastries to a rack until cool enough to eat. These can be eaten warm or at room temperature.

Cooking ahead of time: You can make the filling up to 1 day ahead and refrigerate it to fill the turnovers later.

Storage: These turnovers will keep in the refrigerator for up to 4 days. To reheat, wrap in foil and bake 8 to 10 minutes in a 350°F. oven, or until heated through.

Seafood

MOM'S OWN FISH STICKS

Makes about 8 fish sticks

I was beginning to despair of ever developing a home-made fish stick that is as good as the frozen kind I grew up with and loved. Finally, after at least a dozen attempts, I decided to try this wheat germ–sesame seed coating and —WOW!—I had a winner. They don't taste exactly like the frozen Friday-night fish sticks, but they're very crispy and just as delicious—without all the additives.

¼ cup bread crumbs

¼ cup wheat germ

¼ cup sesame seeds

1 teaspoon paprika

¼ teaspoon salt

1 egg

1 tablespoon water

¾ pound flounder, sole, *or* whitefish fillets, cut into strips

The Old Standby

In addition to the staple sandwich, try tuna on whole wheat bread or a whole wheat waffle with cheese melted on top. Simon also loves to have his little individual can of tuna, so I buy the pop-top 4-ounce cans for him. At mealtime I peel the top off of one of these cans, drain the liquid, give him the can and a fork, and he's happy.

1. Preheat the oven to 350°F.

2. In a shallow dish, combine the bread crumbs, wheat germ, sesame seeds, paprika, and salt. Put the egg into another shallow dish with the water and beat with a fork to blend thoroughly.

3. Dip the fish pieces into the bread crumb mixture, then dip them into the egg, then again into the bread crumbs.

4. Place the fish strips on a baking sheet coated with nonstick baking spray and bake for 20 minutes, or until the fish is cooked through. Serve when cool enough to eat.

Cooking ahead of time: You can make a batch of the dry coating mixture (bread crumbs, wheat germ, sesame seeds, paprika, salt) and keep it in a covered container in the refrigerator for up to 3 weeks. With this on hand, you can make fish sticks as you need them.

Storage: Once cooked, these fish sticks will last about 3 days in your refrigerator. You can reheat them in the microwave or in a low oven. (Freeze after cooking and reheat in the same way.)

Seafood

SWEET-AND-SOUR SHRIMP

Makes 1¾ cups

Children love Chinese food. Sweet-and-sour dishes have a bad name because they're usually so poorly made in American-Chinese restaurants—not to mention dyed! But if you make it from scratch, sweet-and-sour shrimp is wholesome and delicious.

½ medium red bell pepper, diced (about ¾ cup)
¼ cup chopped onion
1 tablespoon vegetable oil
½ cup diced pineapple (canned without added sugar, *or* fresh)
1¼ cups unsweetened pineapple juice
1 tablespoon reduced-sodium soy sauce
1 tablespoon distilled white vinegar
¼ pound shrimp, peeled (see Hint)

1. In a medium skillet over medium heat, sauté the red pepper and onion in oil for 5 minutes.

2. Add the pineapple, increase the heat, and sauté for 2 minutes. Add the pineapple juice, soy sauce, and vinegar and cook over high heat, stirring, for 4 minutes. Add the shrimp and sauté for 1 more minute. Serve when cool enough to eat, with rice or rice noodles.

Hint: You can use fresh or frozen shrimp for this recipe. Also, the shrimp can be of any size, from the tiniest, fingernail-size shrimp, to large, 4-to-a-pound ones (which you may want to cut into smaller pieces before serving to a small child).

Variations: Make this into sweet-and-sour chicken by substituting boneless and skinless chicken breast for the shrimp. Cut the chicken into small pieces and add in place of the shrimp in step 2, cooking and stirring until it has lost its pink color and is cooked through.

Storage: This will last in the refrigerator for up to 3 days.

SMOOTH FISH MOUSSE

Makes 1½ cups

This is a great recipe for those children who usually refuse to eat fish. It looks smooth and white and tastes creamy. Even if your child doesn't like spicy food, don't worry about the Tabasco in this recipe—you can't taste this tiny amount; it's there just to perk up the flavors.

1¼ cups cold water
⅓ pound flounder, sole, *or* whitefish fillets (enough to
      make ½ cup flaked cooked fish)
½ teaspoon unflavored gelatin
¼ cup boiling water
2 tablespoons mayonnaise
1 teaspoon fresh lemon juice
¾ teaspoon salt
1 dash Tabasco
¼ cup heavy cream

1. In a medium skillet over medium heat, bring 1 cup of the water to a simmer. Add the fish, reduce the heat to medium-low, and cook for about 4 minutes, or until the fish is opaque. Remove with a slotted spoon and let cool to room temperature. Puree the fish in a food processor, adding a bit of the cooking liquid, if necessary.

2. Pour remaining cold water into a medium bowl; sprinkle the gelatin over the water and let stand 2 minutes. Gradually add boiling water and whisk until gelatin is dissolved. Whisk the mayonnaise, lemon juice, salt, and Tabasco into the gelatin, then chill for 20 minutes, or until slightly thickened.

3. Whip the cream until soft peaks are formed.

4. Fold together the pureed fish, thickened gelatin mixture, and whipped cream. Generously coat a 1½-cup bowl or mold with nonstick baking spray (I use a deep, glass cereal bowl for this). Pour the mousse mixture into the bowl, cover with plastic wrap, and refrigerate for at least 4 hours, or until set.

5. To serve, unmold onto a plate and cut into wedges. (You shouldn't have any trouble getting the mousse out of the mold, but if you do, upend the bowl onto a plate and cover the bottom of the bowl with a kitchen towel that you have dipped into hot water and wrung dry; leave it there for 1 minute, and then lift the bowl up neatly.)

Variations: You can also make this with any leftover cooked fish you happen to have; all you need is ½ cup of cooked, pureed fish—it could even be canned tuna or salmon.

If you'd like to get fancy, make this in a mold that is shaped like a fish—or any other shape, for that matter; I've got some gelatin molds that are shaped like animals that I sometimes use. Just make sure that you've coated the mold well with nonstick baking spray.

For grown-up kids: If you are making this for an older child, or for grown-ups, or you'd like a little more flavor, add 1 minced tablespoon of your favorite fresh herb, such as parsley, chives, or dill.

Storage: This will keep for 1 week in your refrigerator.

ORZO WITH TOMATOES AND RED SNAPPER

Makes 1 adult or 2 child's servings

Three-year-old Olympia has very adventurous taste buds, probably because both of her parents are chefs. Her mom, Helen Chardack, has created inspired dishes like this one just for her.

½ cup orzo
2 tablespoons chopped onion
2 tablespoons diced yellow summer squash
1 teaspoon minced red bell pepper
½ teaspoon chopped fresh parsley
1 teaspoon olive oil
4 canned plum tomatoes, drained and chopped
½ teaspoon reduced-sodium soy sauce
1 tablespoon water
Salt and pepper to taste
4 ounces red snapper fillet

A Fishy Lunch

If you have some fish left over from last night's dinner, make a fish salad just as you would fix canned tuna: Mash the fish with mayonnaise (lowfat or regular), celery, and pickle relish (or whatever your family's traditional mixture is). Serve it on bread or crackers, or use endive or romaine leaves to scoop it up.

1. Cook the orzo according to package directions. Drain and keep warm.

2. Over medium heat in a small skillet, sauté the onion, squash, red pepper, and parsley in the olive oil for 2 minutes. Add the tomatoes, soy sauce, and water. Cook, stirring, for 1 minute. Season with salt and pepper.

3. Place the fish in the pan on top of the vegetables and spoon some of the vegetables over the fish. Cover and cook over low heat until fillet is cooked, about 5 minutes.

4. Place the orzo in a shallow serving dish and spoon the cooked fish and vegetables over the pasta.

Variation: This dish can be made with any other white-fleshed fish fillet, such as flounder, sole, or whitefish.

Cooking ahead of time: You can cook a batch of orzo and keep it, covered, in the refrigerator for about 5 days, using it during the week for last-minute cold or hot meals; it reheats well in the microwave. Toss the pasta with a couple teaspoons of olive oil or vegetable oil before putting it away, so it doesn't dry out. (This works well for any other type of pasta, for that matter.)

Storage: This will keep for 2 days in the refrigerator.

JIMMY SCHMIDT'S SCALLOPS WITH RED TARTAR SAUCE

Makes 4 servings

Jimmy Schmidt, owner of the popular Rattlesnake Club restaurant in Detroit, has two small children: Stephen, who is three years old, and Taylor, one year old. Both of his kids like the dish their father concocted for them.

1¼ cups corn oil
1 small taro root, peeled and finely julienned
Salt to taste
2 cups all-purpose flour
1 tablespoon mild paprika
1 pound large sea scallops
1 recipe Red Tartar Sauce (recipe follows)

Seafood

1. In a medium skillet over medium-high heat, heat 1 cup of the corn oil. Rinse the taro under cold running water until the water is clear. Drain well, then dry with paper toweling. Add the taro to the oil and fry until golden, about 2 minutes. Remove with a slotted spoon to paper towels to drain. Keep warm in a low oven. Salt to taste.

2. In a medium bowl, combine the flour and paprika. Add the scallops, stirring to coat with the flour mixture. Remove the scallops and shake to remove excess flour.

3. In a large nonstick skillet over high heat, heat the remaining ¼ cup oil. Add the scallops and cook until browned and well seared, about 2 minutes. Turn over and cook until slightly firm, about 1 minute, depending on the size. Remove to paper towels to drain.

4. To serve, position the taro chips across the serving plate. Arrange the scallops across the chips. Pass the Red Tartar Sauce to be drizzled over everything at the table.

Note: After cooking, the scallops can be cut into smaller pieces if the children are young.

Storage: The cooked scallops and taro will keep for 1 day in the refrigerator, but will lose most of their crispness.

🔲 **X2** 🕴

RED TARTAR SAUCE

Makes 2 cups

1 large egg yolk
1 teaspoon Dijon mustard
¼ cup fresh lemon juice
1 cup corn oil
2 tablespoons sweet relish, drained
2 tablespoons diced dill pickle
2 tablespoons capers, drained and minced
1 tablespoon minced fresh parsley
½ cup ketchup *or* mild barbecue sauce
Salt to taste

In the bowl of a mixer, combine the egg yolk, mustard, and lemon juice. On high speed, gradually add the corn oil in a steady stream. On slow speed, mix in the remaining ingredients. Adjust salt to taste. Refrigerate until ready to use.

Storage: This sauce will last for 5 days in the refrigerator.

MEATLESS MEALS

Many foods in our diet offer protein as complete and nutritious as meat, and some of them are well known, like cheese, eggs, and nuts. Others, like tofu (or any other preparation of soybeans) or bean-and-grain combinations, are not as much a part of American food culture as they are in other countries. I feel that feeding Simon from babyhood is a good opportunity to teach healthful food customs that will last his lifetime, even if they aren't the ones I grew up with (my family's Tuesday-night steak dinners would have supplied a Chinese family with protein for a year). In my house, we rely on some of the following recipes—and those that are in the same genre—for *our* routine meals.

CHEESY BEANS

Makes 2 cups

Lima beans have gotten a bum rap in this country, probably because they are prepared so badly in school cafeterias. A good lima bean is sweet and delicious, something like a combination of peas and corn. This recipe is a one-dish meal because it has vegetables (lima beans are full of nutrients), protein (cheese and nuts), and a grain (the rolled-oats topping). Pine nuts are one of the few whole nuts children can eat before the age of five, because they are so soft and won't cause choking, and their rich flavor is enticing.

1 cup frozen baby lima beans, thawed (about half a 10-
ounce package; see Hint)
⅓ cup minced onion
¼ cup grated cheddar cheese
¼ cup pine nuts (pignoli)
½ cup chicken broth
½ tablespoon reduced-sodium soy sauce
½ cup quick-cooking rolled oats
1 tablespoon unsalted butter

Pimiento Cheese, Y'all

While traveling in Georgia, I discovered from my native Georgian friends that there are parts of the South where children eat something they call *pimennacheese* (all one word), just as other American children eat peanut butter and jelly. It's a mixture of grated cheese, mayonnaise, and diced canned pimiento, spread on bread or crackers. It's especially easy to make with the assistance of a food processor.

1. Preheat the oven to 350°F. Coat a round 8- or 9-inch cake pan with nonstick baking spray. (If you have a decorative heatproof casserole dish that holds the same amount, you can use that.)

2. Mix the lima beans, onion, cheese, and nuts and spoon into the prepared pan. Mix the broth and soy sauce, and pour into the pan. Evenly sprinkle the oats over the top and lightly press it down; dot with butter. Bake for 35 minutes, or until the top is golden brown.

Hint: Thaw the lima beans in the microwave, or by putting them in the refrigerator for a few hours or overnight.

Variation: If you'd rather not use lima beans, substitute fresh zucchini cut into ½-inch chunks.

Cooking ahead of time: You can make up the casserole and refrigerate it for a day before cooking. Add the oats topping and bake it just before mealtime, adding 5 minutes to the baking time if it's just been taken out of the refrigerator.

Storage: This will keep in the refrigerator for 5 days. You can reheat it in a low oven or in the microwave.

❄ **X2** 🚶 🛒

BEANS AND RICE

Makes 6 cups

Almost every nation in the world has a beans-and-rice dish as part of its national cuisine, and for good reason: the combination makes a protein that is just as nutritious and complete as meat, and for a lot less money. Cubans, for example, eat black beans and rice (the nickname for this dish translates as "Christians and Moors"). The American version of this worldwide favorite is southern, called simply red beans and rice, and it's usually fiery hot from the addition of hot peppers or hot sauce.

This is a master recipe to make beans and rice for children. It's slightly sweet-and-sour, and you can use any kind of beans you like: red, black, white, or pinto. The recipe is especially easy because it's made with canned beans. As one of the best cooks I know, Shirley Glaser, says, "After a lifetime of cooking beans in every way imaginable, I've decided that you can never make them taste as good as they do when they come out of a can."

1 medium red, yellow, *or* green bell pepper
1 medium onion
1 Granny Smith apple
2 garlic cloves
2 tablespoons vegetable oil
1 (16-ounce) can beans, including liquid (see Hint)
1 tablespoon molasses
1½ tablespoons balsamic *or* red wine vinegar
¼ teaspoon ground cumin
3 cups cooked brown or white rice, warmed
½ cup sour cream or plain yogurt

Beans, Beans– the Musical Fruit

I recently spoke to a man in his fifties who grew up in South Carolina, and he said he had never tasted peanut butter until he was in his twenties, in the Army. This surprised me, so I asked him what his mother fed him for a staple lunch when he was growing up. This is what he described: cooked beans mashed with mayonnaise spread on whole wheat toast.

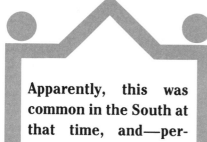

Apparently, this was common in the South at that time, and—perhaps unwittingly—the combination of beans and toast make a complete protein, just as nutritious as meat or fish. It sounded delicious, so I made it for Simon and me for lunch. I drained one 16-ounce can of kidney beans, mashed them with a fork, and mixed them with a little mayonnaise. For variety, sometimes I add a little grated cheese and minced scallions.

1. Peel, core, and seed (as appropriate) the bell pepper, onion, apple, and garlic, and chop into large pieces. Put into a food processor and mince together.

2. In a medium skillet over medium heat, sauté the minced vegetables in the oil for 10 minutes, stirring occasionally, until the liquid has evaporated.

3. Stir in the beans (with liquid), molasses, vinegar, and cumin. Cook for 5 minutes more, stirring occasionally, or until beans are heated through. Serve beans over rice and garnish with sour cream or yogurt.

Hint: Since canned beans are packed with salt, I haven't called for extra salt in the recipe. You might like to add some, according to taste.

Variations: Sometimes I can find frozen diced green bell peppers in my supermarket, which work perfectly in this recipe. If you'd like to use them, substitute 1 cup frozen diced green peppers for the fresh; defrost the peppers slightly, grind them in the food processor with the other ingredients, and proceed with the recipe.

If you haven't already done so, investigate the canned bean section of your supermarket to find the kind of beans you'd like to use in this recipe. Depending on which part of the country you live in, that section might also be where the Spanish and Mexican foods are kept. Some beans to consider are kidney beans (red), Great Northern beans (white), black beans, Roman beans (mottled pink and white), and so on—there seem to be endless varieties. Make sure the can you buy is packed with nothing more than water and salt (and perhaps calcium chloride or some other natural preservative).

(continued on next page)

Meatless Meals

This is a good recipe to use with the rice that is inevitably left over from a Chinese take-out dinner. (We always ask for brown rice when we order Chinese food.) You could also serve it with couscous, which takes only 5 minutes to cook.

For grown-up kids: Grown-ups who are in the mood can add hot sauce or hot peppers to this dish.

Storage: The beans will last for about a week in the refrigerator. You can heat them in the microwave or over low heat.

Good Food Comes in Small Packages

John Mariani, food writer and author of *The Dictionary of American Food and Drink,* is the father of two young boys who always seem to prefer food served in small packages. One of their favorites is *shu mai—* filled Chinese dumplings that are available frozen in supermarkets, and can be boiled in soup or sautéed until brown and crispy.

BABY EGG ROLLS

Makes 20 egg rolls

Simon adores these baby egg rolls, and even ate one in his television debut. I made a batch of them on Live with Regis and Kathie Lee, *and fed them to a tasting panel of six babies in high chairs—Simon and five of his friends. Fortunately for me, they devoured them on cue.*

You can find egg roll wrappers (and wonton wrappers) in the produce section of your supermarket, along with the tofu.

¼ cup minced scallions (green and white parts)
1 teaspoon minced fresh ginger
4 tablespoons vegetable oil
1 cup diced carrots
½ cup bean sprouts or diced celery
½ cup frozen chopped spinach, thawed and drained
¼ cup chicken broth
2 tablespoons reduced-sodium soy sauce
1 tablespoon sugar
4 ounces soft *or* firm tofu
10 egg roll wrappers, each cut in half diagonally, *or* 20
    wonton wrappers

1. In a wok or skillet, sauté the scallions and ginger in 2 tablespoons of the oil over low heat, stirring occasionally, for about 10 minutes, or until the scallions are translucent and wilted.

(continued on next page)

2. Add the carrots and bean sprouts or celery and stir-fry over high heat for 2 minutes. Add the spinach, broth, soy sauce, and sugar; bring to a boil, then reduce heat and simmer for 10 to 15 minutes, stirring occasionally, until the vegetables are soft. Cool for at least 15 minutes. Place the mixture in a food processor along with the tofu and grind to the desired texture.

3. Fill and roll the egg roll wrappers according to the diagram, using 1 tablespoon of filling for each roll. Pour the remaining 2 tablespoons of vegetable oil into a skillet and sauté the egg rolls over medium-high heat until golden brown on all sides, using tongs to turn them. Serve when cool enough to eat.

Variations: Substitute any kind of fresh or frozen vegetables for this recipe—simply make sure the volume adds up to the same as called for here. The craftiest thing to do is to use the vegetables your child won't touch ordinarily, since he won't be able to identify them in this form.

Another extremely simple way to make egg roll filling is to use leftover Chinese food, either vegetables or a meat-and-vegetable combination. Grind it in the food processor with or without some tofu, and follow the filling and sautéing instructions here.

Cooking ahead of time: You can make the filling up to 2 days ahead, and fill and sauté the egg rolls as you need them.

For grown-up kids: The size of these egg rolls is perfect for hors d'oeuvres. For regulation-size egg rolls, don't cut the wrappers in half.

Fast Food from the Far East

Tofu (bean curd) is an ideal food for children. They love the texture and taste—or lack of it, since it's consummately bland. Tofu is high in protein and calcium, and can be tolerated by children who are allergic to milk and milk products. (It shouldn't be given to children who are allergic to soybeans, obviously, and one in every five people allergic to milk is also allergic to soybeans.) Firm or extra-firm tofu can be cut neatly, but soft tofu can be cut into cubes as well, if that's the only kind available.

Tofu is sold in the produce section of most supermarkets or in health food stores. To store, remove the tofu from its original container and place it in a large bowl and cover with cold water. Change the water daily. The tofu will keep for two weeks in the refrigerator.

One way I serve tofu is to skewer extra-firm tofu cubes and avocado cubes alternately on a chopstick. I serve these with whole wheat breadsticks and a dip made from yogurt mixed with fresh herbs, to make a complete meal.

1. Place filling diagonally on wrapper.

2. Fold corner over filling.

3. Fold up both sides. Moisten edges of last flap.

4. Roll over until flap is completely wound around.

SHERÉE'S VEGGIE CASSEROLE

Makes about 4 cups

This is a favorite dish in Sherée Hernandez's family, from Boise, Idaho. Sherée lived with us as Simon's nanny until he was two years old, and in that time this dish became one of our family favorites, too. Sometimes Simon calls this "quiche," which is not far off the mark, since it resembles a quiche without the crust.

1 (10-ounce) package frozen chopped broccoli
1 (10-ounce) package frozen cauliflower florets
1 cup crushed saltine crackers
½ cup (4 ounces) sour cream
½ cup (4 ounces) cottage cheese
½ cup condensed cream of mushroom soup
3 tablespoons minced onion (optional)
⅓ cup (about 1½ ounces) shredded cheddar cheese

1. Take the frozen broccoli and cauliflower out of their boxes, place in separate microwavable bowls, and microwave on high for 15 minutes. When cool enough to handle, chop the cauliflower into small pieces.

2. Preheat the oven to 350°F. Coat the inside surfaces of an 8- or 9-inch round or square cake pan with nonstick baking spray.

3. In a large bowl, mix the crushed saltines, sour cream, cottage cheese, mushroom soup, and onion, if using.

4. Put the broccoli and cauliflower into the bottom of the prepared cake pan and cover with the sour cream mixture. Top with the grated cheese and bake for 30 minutes, until cheese is melted and bubbly. Serve when cool enough to eat.

Variation: You can use other vegetables for this casserole, such as potatoes, fennel, carrots, turnips, corn, and cabbage. If you are using other vegetables or a combination of other vegetables, use the same volume as called for here, cut the vegetables into bite-size pieces, and microwave, steam, or boil until almost completely cooked before adding to the casserole.

To reduce the fat and cholesterol content: Use low-fat cottage cheese and a sour cream substitute.

Cooking ahead of time: Assemble the casserole completely (eliminate the onion in this case) and refrigerate it for up to a day ahead, then bake it just before serving; add 10 minutes to the baking time if you take the casserole out of the refrigerator just before baking.

Storage: The cooked casserole will keep for 2 days in the refrigerator.

X2

TORTILLA PIE

Makes one 6-inch pie

You could call this a Mexican lasagna, only it's much easier to make. The texture is soft enough for little mouths, and it has a very mild flavor.

2 cups mixed frozen vegetables, thawed (see Hints)
¼ cup chopped onion
¾ cup tomato puree *or* sauce
1 teaspoon chili powder (see Hints)
¼ teaspoon salt
3 corn tortillas
½ cup (about 2 ounces) grated Muenster cheese

1. Preheat the oven to 375°F. Coat an 8- or 9-inch round or square cake pan with nonstick baking spray.

2. Put the vegetables, onion, ½ cup of the tomato purée or sauce, chili powder, and salt into a food processor and grind until mixture is pureed.

3. Place 1 tortilla on the bottom of the cake pan. Spread half of the vegetable mixture to the edges of the tortilla and top with the second tortilla. Spread with the remaining vegetable mixture and top with the third tortilla. Spread this tortilla with the remaining ¼ cup tomato puree or sauce and sprinkle with the cheese. Cover pan with foil and bake for 20 minutes, or until the cheese has melted and the pie is heated through.

Mexican Breakfast

Sometimes I make a special breakfast for Simon by wrapping scrambled eggs in a tortilla, which he likes to dip into a little side dish of ketchup.

Meatless Meals

Hints: I use mixed frozen vegetables, but you can use one or more of the following: corn, carrots, green peas, and green beans.

There are 2 kinds of chili powder sold in jars in the supermarket—"hot" and plain. If you are making this for babies or children, be sure to buy the latter.

Cooking ahead of time: You can make this up completely and refrigerate it for up to 24 hours; when it's time for dinner, simply pop it in the oven for 20 minutes (add 5 minutes to the cooking time if it's taken directly out of the refrigerator).

For grown-up kids: Those who want to raise the thermostat can add hot sauce at the table.

Storage: This will keep in the refrigerator for up to a week. You can reheat it by covering the pan with foil and putting it in a 300°F. oven until it's heated through.

❄ **X2** 🚶 🍼

VEGETABLE HAND-ROLLS

Makes about 4 hand-rolls

These are modeled after the fish and vegetable hand-rolls served at sushi bars in Japanese restaurants. Seaweed is full of calcium and iron, and the crisp texture of nori *is very appealing to toddlers and children. Kids love to eat hand-rolls because they can hold them like ice cream cones and nibble away.*

½ cup brown rice (short grain, if you can find it)

1¼ cups water

2 tablespoons rice vinegar (see Hints)

2 teaspoons granulated brown *or* white sugar

1 teaspoon salt

½ cup peeled and julienned vegetables, such as carrot,
    cucumber, summer squash, turnip, white radish,
    bell pepper, lettuce (see Hints)

2 sheets *nori* (toasted seaweed; see Hints)

1. Put the rice in a strainer and rinse under tap water for a minute or so. Place rice and water in a small, heavy pot and bring to a boil; reduce heat to low and cover the pot tightly. Cook for 40 minutes, or until rice is tender.

2. Place the vinegar, sugar, and salt in a tiny saucepan and heat for a few seconds over high heat, until sugar and salt are dissolved. (You can do this in a microwave, too.) When the rice is cooked, place it in a small mixing bowl and combine with the vinegar mixture; mix well.

3. With a sharp knife, cut the *nori* sheets in half. Lay a sheet on a plate and cover with a generous ¼ cup of the rice mixture. With dampened fingers, spread the rice to cover most of the *nori* (neatness is not important). Lay a few strips of vegetable over the rice, then roll up the *nori* into the shape of an ice cream cone. Eat immediately. Make the rest of the hand-rolls in the same way.

Hints: *Nori* sheets are found in health food stores or stores that specialize in Japanese foods. They can be mail-ordered from Katagiri, 224 East 59th Street, New York, N.Y. 10022; (212) 755-3566.

Rice vinegar, which has a gentle flavor and is slightly sweet, is available in supermarkets. There is a product called sushi vinegar, which is sold under the Sushi Chef label of the Baycliff company; it already contains sugar and salt, so omit those ingredients if you use it. I like to use brown rice vinegar, which I buy at the health food store.

The measurement of the vegetables is only approximate. The exact amount depends on how much you decide to put into each hand-roll.

Variations: You can also use white rice for this recipe, which should be cooked without additional flavorings and then mixed with the vinegar-sugar-salt mixture. I recommend converted rice, since it has more vitamins than regular white rice.

(continued on next page)

You can also use avocado to fill these hand-rolls, but they should be cut into ½-inch-wide strips.

In addition to the vegetables, you can fill these with shrimp, or with *surimi* (sea legs), which is fish pressed to resemble crab meat.

Instead of *nori,* you can use crisp lettuce leaves (such as Boston) to wrap the rice and vegetables.

You might also like to sprinkle sesame seeds over the rice before adding the vegetables.

Cooking ahead of time: The rice can be made up to 24 hours ahead, refrigerated, and brought back to room temperature—or slightly warmed in the microwave or on top of the stove—before serving. The assembling of the hand-rolls should be done just before serving; grownups and older children might like to make their own hand-rolls from an array of vegetables.

For grown-up kids: Grown-ups might like to dip their hand-rolls into a half-and-half mixture of reduced-sodium soy sauce and rice vinegar, with a few minced scallions sprinkled on top.

X2

VEGGIES

You can have a cookie if you eat all of your vegetables. Before Simon was born, I swore that I would never stoop to bribery to get my child to eat what's good for him. But sometimes, when days have gone by and not a vegetable has passed Simon's lips, I get desperate, and am willing to try any trick that works. "Don't worry," said my pediatrician, "as long as he eats a green vegetable and a yellow vegetable every day, then you're fine." Surely you're joking, I responded silently. In my more rational moments, I collected a group of recipes that Simon likes, and I pass them on here.

RED CABBAGE AND APPLE HASH

Makes 3 cups

This is one of my favorite dishes. I decided to make it for Simon when racking my brain for ways to get him to eat vegetables. He loved it; the sweet-sour flavor is enticing for all babies and children, and the red cabbage contains a great deal of vitamin C.

½ cup minced onion

2 tablespoons vegetable oil

½ medium head red cabbage

1 apple, peeled and cored

1 cup chicken broth

¼ cup frozen unsweetened grape juice concentrate (see Hint)

3 tablespoons fresh lemon juice

1 teaspoon salt

1 cup sour cream or plain yogurt (optional)

1. In a medium skillet over medium heat, sauté the onion in the oil for 10 minutes.

2. In the meantime, cut out the core of the cabbage and discard, then cut the cabbage into chunks. Put the chunks into the food processor along with the apple and process until minced.

3. Add the cabbage and apple to the skillet along with the broth, grape juice, lemon juice, and salt and bring to a boil. Reduce the heat to a simmer, cover the pan, and cook, stirring occasionally, for 25 minutes. If the hash is still a bit too liquid at this point, remove the cover and reduce over high heat until the desired consistency is reached. Serve when cool enough to eat, or, if you like, cool the hash for 10 minutes, then stir in the sour cream or yogurt before serving, if using.

Hint: The grape juice concentrate can be thawed before you measure out ¼ cup, then you can put it in an airtight plastic container and refreeze it until you need it again.

For grown-up kids: Slice the cabbage thinly instead of grinding it.

Storage: This keeps well in the refrigerator for 1 week. In fact, it is one of those stewed dishes that gets better with time.

X2

VEGETABLES IN NIGHTGOWNS

Makes about 12 pieces

Fritters are a venerable American specialty. They're really nothing more than bite-size pieces of food coated with pancake batter. Babies and children adore them.

   These fritters are great warm and surprisingly good cold, which makes them good picnic food as well.

2 quarts vegetable oil
⅓ cup whole wheat flour
½ teaspoon baking powder
½ teaspoon salt
¼ cup plus 2 tablespoons milk, or more as needed
1 egg yolk
12 bite-size pieces of vegetables, such as broccoli florets,
      cauliflower florets, mushrooms, summer squash
      rounds, carrot rounds, sweet potato slices, asparagus
      tips, green beans, eggplant cubes, kohlrabi rounds,
      whole okra pods (don't cut off stem end or the okra
      will get slimy), red or green bell pepper squares

Sneaky Veggie Tricks

■ **If your child won't touch vegetables, mix finely grated raw carrots with chunky peanut butter and use as a spread for crackers or bread.**

■ **Puree a raw egg or two with some cooked (or frozen and defrosted) vegetables in a blender; cook the mixture in the same way as you make scrambled eggs.**

■ **A professional chef in Lapland, of all places, told me how he gets his children to eat vegetables as well as the meat or fish they are served** for dinner. They are given vegetables as a separate first course, and then comes the meat or fish, as the second course, to be eaten after the vegetables are finished.

■ My friend Carol Hall used to give her children something she called "Carrot Juice Hiding in Orange Juice" every morning with breakfast. She mixed one-third carrot juice in a glass of o.j., and the kids drank it down. I do this sometimes with fresh carrot juice I've made myself, or with unadulterated carrot juice I buy in cans in the supermarket.

1. Place the oil in a heavy, medium pot or an electric frying pan and heat to 375°F.

2. Whisk together all the remaining ingredients except the vegetables. If the batter seems to be a bit thick, whisk in more milk. (You can mix the batter in the blender, if you like.)

3. Dip vegetable pieces into the batter and let excess batter drip off for a few seconds. Carefully drop vegetables into the hot oil and cook, turning gently with tongs, until golden brown (time will vary from vegetable to vegetable; generally it takes from 2 to 5 minutes). Drain on paper towels and serve when cool enough to eat.

Note: The secret to making these crisp and light is to regulate the temperature of the oil so that it remains constantly at 375°F. and not to crowd the pan. A thermometer is highly recommended for this task. The easiest method of all, however, is to use an electric appliance that automatically regulates the temperature, such as an electric frying pan or a deep-fryer.

Variation: Make fritters out of tofu cubes (use firm or extra-firm tofu).

Storage: The raw batter can be kept in the refrigerator for a day or so. The cooked fritters will also keep for about a day in the refrigerator.

▦ **X2** 朩 🛒

Veggies

QUESADILLAS

Makes 4 small wedges

Tortillas are a delicious and healthful alternative to bread and crackers, and now they're readily available in almost all supermarkets, usually in the dairy case. (If you want to warm plain tortillas, wrap them in damp paper towels and microwave for a few seconds.) This is more of a snack, but it contains some hidden veggies inside.

1 flour *or* corn tortilla
2 tablespoons (about ½ ounce) grated cheddar cheese
1 tablespoon minced red, green, *or* yellow bell pepper

1. Place the tortilla on a dinner plate. Sprinkle the cheese and minced pepper on half the tortilla. Fold the tortilla in half over the topping.

2. Microwave for 30 seconds, or until the cheese is melted. Cut into 4 wedges and serve when cool enough to eat.

Variations: You can also heat this in a toaster oven or under a broiler, just until the cheese is melted.

If you have any bits of leftover meat or fish, you can also mince these to add to the cheese. Sliced avocado can also be used.

Any hard or semihard cheese can be substituted for the cheddar in this recipe: Monterey Jack, mozzarella, Swiss.

X2 ⫯Å

When All Else Fails

Make a grilled cheese sandwich. Best when made with real American or cheddar cheese, not cheese spread. Or make a toasted cheese sandwich in the toaster oven. In either case, these sandwiches are more fun to eat when cut into cubes or triangles, or cut into shapes with cookie cutters.

ALMOST-CHINESE BROCCOLI

Makes 1 cup

When Simon couldn't stand to eat other vegetables, he would still gobble up this broccoli dish. We didn't even have to call them "trees," as some parents do. The flavor is similar to, but milder than, the broccoli you get in Chinese restaurants.

1 cup broccoli florets
3 tablespoons chicken broth *or* water
1 tablespoon minced onion
1 teaspoon reduced-sodium soy sauce

1. Put all the ingredients into a medium saucepan; cover, bring to a boil, then reduce heat to low and steam until broccoli is tender—about 10 minutes total cooking time.

2. Serve when cool enough to eat.

Storage: The broccoli will keep in the refrigerator for 4 days, and can be reheated slowly over low heat or in the microwave.

🔲 **X2** 🧍 🛒

Veggies

BABY GANOUJ

Makes about 2 cups puree

Under the name baba ganouj, *this Middle Eastern eggplant puree has a subtle yet haunting smoky flavor. Babies and children love the combination of seasonings (including sesame) and the smooth texture.*

This is delicious as a spread or dip for pita (try to use little pitas—"pitettes"—sometimes sold in supermarkets) or vegetables (the vegetables should be cooked, if your child is younger than three). Children like baba ganouj *spread on a piece of bread.*

1 medium eggplant (about 1 pound)
½ cup parsley leaves
1 small garlic clove
⅓ cup sesame butter (tahini; see Hint)
⅓ cup fresh lemon juice
2 tablespoons olive oil
Salt and freshly ground pepper to taste

1. Preheat the oven to 350°F.

2. Place the eggplant on a cookie sheet or cake pan and bake for 1 hour and 20 minutes, or until it begins to collapse. (It will collapse even more when you remove it from the oven and it starts to cool.)

Saves on Dishwashing, Too

Some children love to use endive leaves as edible scoops for chopped-up foods.

3. When cool enough to handle, cut off the stem end of the cooked eggplant and discard, then slip off the skin using your fingers and discard. Place the eggplant flesh in a food processor, along with the remaining ingredients (including the eggplant juices that have collected in the baking pan) and puree until very smooth. Correct the seasoning—you will need a generous amount of salt and perhaps more lemon juice. Serve at room temperature.

Hint: Sesame butter (tahini) is like peanut butter, only made with sesame seeds. You can find it in health food stores, often sold in bulk, and in some supermarkets in the ethnic foods section, where it is sold for Middle Eastern dishes.

Variation: You can also spread this on a plain broiled chicken breast or a broiled fillet of fish, to add a little interest and flavor.

Cooking ahead of time: The eggplant can be baked up to a day ahead (in the evening, perhaps, when you're cleaning up the kitchen) and held, tightly covered, in the refrigerator until you're ready to make the puree.

For grown-up kids: If you're making this for adults, add 2 or 3 more garlic cloves.

Storage: This can be covered and refrigerated for up to 5 days.

🕧 **X2** 🚶 🛒

PAPRIKA POTATOES

Makes about 1½ cups

This is a staple dish in George's native Hungary, where paprika is widely used. Paprika is one of the best-known sources of vitamin C; in fact, it was in peppers that vitamin C was first discovered.

1 tablespoon minced onion
2 teaspoons vegetable oil
1 tablespoon minced green or red bell pepper *or* Italian
    frying pepper
1 medium potato, peeled and cut into ½-inch cubes
½ teaspoon Hungarian sweet paprika (see Hint)
½ teaspoon tomato paste
Salt and freshly ground pepper to taste

1. In a small, heavy skillet over medium heat, sauté the onion in the oil for 3 minutes. Add the pepper and sauté for 3 more minutes. Add the potato and sauté for 3 more minutes.

2. Remove the skillet from the heat and add the paprika; stir to mix well. Add the tomato paste, salt and pepper, and enough water to barely cover the potato.

"Welcome to My Kitchen, May I Help You?"

My ingenious friend Harriet Bell makes homemade french fries by cutting potatoes into sticks, tossing them with a small amount of vegetable oil, and baking them in a 400°F. oven for about 40 minutes, or until golden brown. She and her six-year-old son, David, use them to play McDonald's. She stands behind the kitchen counter and her son walks up to "order" dinner from her: french fries, Chicken Nuggets (page 76), and a milkshake.

3. Return the pot to the stove over high heat; bring to a boil, reduce heat to medium-low, cover pot, and cook for 10 minutes, or until potato is cooked through. Serve when cool enough to eat.

Hint: Paprika, as it's used in Hungary, bears no resemblance to the paprika we find on most supermarket spice shelves, which is usually imported from Spain and tasteless, used to sprinkle over eggs or fish to give a smidgeon of color. The real paprika, the kind that should be used in this recipe, is available in many supermarkets in red tins under the Szeged brand. It's sweet, rich, and full of vitamin C. Large quantities (one pound minimum) to use in authentic goulash soups and Hungarian stews, can be ordered from Paprikas Weiss, 1546 Second Avenue, New York, N.Y. 10028; (212) 288-6117.

Variations: Hungarians often add cooked and sliced sausage, frankfurters, or ham to this dish at the end of the cooking time. For the amount of potato in this recipe, you would add about 1/3 cup sliced cooked meat.

For grown-up kids: Cut the potatoes into larger chunks (which will probably lengthen the cooking time somewhat).

Storage: This will keep well in the refrigerator for 3 days. Like all stews, it will get a little better with age. Reheat in a microwave or over low heat on top of the stove.

X2

CARROT AND SWEET POTATO TSIMMES

Makes about 3 cups

Whenever I mention tsimmes to someone who is Jewish, he or she says, "My grandma's was the best." My friend Bryna added, "Tsimmes is the star of Jewish cooking." Even if your grandmother didn't make it, it's still a delicious and very nutritious dish.

1 small sweet potato, peeled and cut into chunks
2 medium carrots, peeled and cut into chunks
⅓ cup dried fruit, such as raisins, apricots, dates, prunes, apples, or a mixture
¼ cup orange juice
½ teaspoon grated orange zest
Pinch of ground cinnamon
2 teaspoons unsalted butter

1. Preheat the oven to 350°F. Coat an 8-inch round cake pan (or any other baking pan that holds about the same amount) with nonstick baking spray.

Sweet Potatoes for My Sweetie

I bake sweet potatoes in the microwave for 6 to 10 minutes, depending on how big they are, and mash the flesh with a fork or in the food processor with melted butter and/or Parmesan cheese. Sometimes I peel the whole baked potatoes and cut them into ½-inch rounds, which Simon eats cold as a treat.

2. Put the sweet potato and carrot chunks into a medium saucepan and cover with water. Bring to a boil and cook for 8 minutes, or until tender when pierced with a fork. Drain and rinse with cold running water.

3. Put the cooked sweet potato and carrots into the bowl of a food processor and add the dried fruit. Process until finely chopped. Add the orange juice, orange zest, and cinnamon and process until well blended.

4. Spoon the mixture into the cake pan and smooth the top. Dot the top of the mixture with the butter. Bake for 35 minutes. Serve when cool enough to eat. This can also be refrigerated and eaten cold.

Cooking ahead of time: You can make up the casserole and refrigerate it for a day before cooking. Bake it just before mealtime, adding 5 minutes to the baking time if it's just been taken out of the refrigerator.

Storage: This will keep in your refrigerator for up to 1 week.

WARM EGGPLANT SALAD

Makes about 1 cup

This, devised by Helen Chardack, is really more of a vegetable side dish (or vegetarian main dish) than a salad, but whatever it's called, it's a delicious way to eat eggplant.

½ small eggplant (about 6 ounces)
1 garlic clove, crushed
1 tablespoon olive oil
¼ cup diced red onion
¼ cup tomato sauce
¾ teaspoon sherry vinegar
¼ cup water
2 teaspoons chopped fresh parsley
½ teaspoon dried oregano
½ teaspoon dried thyme
Salt and pepper to taste

1. Peel the eggplant and cut into ½-inch cubes. Cook in a generous amount of boiling salted water for 3 minutes. Drain.

2. Sauté the garlic in a small skillet in the olive oil over medium heat for 1 minute. Remove the garlic and discard. Add the onion and sauté over medium-low heat until light brown, about 5 minutes. Add the eggplant and the remaining ingredients. Cook, stirring occasionally, over medium heat for 10 minutes. Serve warm or at room temperature.

Storage: This will keep for 2 days in the refrigerator; bring it to room temperature before serving.

X2

They're Not Just for Halloween

All of the winter squash varieties—acorn, butternut, pumpkin—are delicious and they're in the market year-round. I put a whole one into the microwave and cook it for 10 to 15 minutes, or until a knife easily pierces the shell. Then I scoop out the flesh and mash it with melted butter and granulated brown sugar or honey. Sometimes I cut the cooked squash into fingers, peel off the skin, and then sprinkle some grated Parmesan cheese on top and microwave them for a few seconds more to melt the cheese.

A winter squash puree is one of the best frozen products available in the supermarket —it doesn't have anything in it except the cooked squash. When I'm in a hurry, I defrost one of those packages in the microwave and stir in some brown sugar or honey.

DREW NIEPORENT'S GUACAMOLE, FOR ANDREW

Makes 3 cups

Drew Nieporent, owner of the acclaimed Montrachet restaurant and Tribeca Grill in New York City, has a four-year-old named Andrew who is a picky eater; in spite of that, he has always loved avocados, so Drew devised this recipe. Andrew says, "No jalapeños, please!"

3 ripe avocados, peeled and pits discarded
1 peeled mild green chili (no seeds, fresh *or* canned),
    chopped
2 tablespoons lime juice
1 teaspoon salt
1 medium tomato, peeled, seeded, and chopped
1 small onion, chopped
1 bunch cilantro (Chinese parsley), chopped
Unsalted blue corn chips

1. Mash the avocados by hand until chunky. Add the next six ingredients and stir until blended.

2. Serve with the corn chips.

Storage: This should be eaten the same day it's made.

🔲 **X2** 🚶 👶

Riverdale Public Library District

BREADS, MUFFINS, AND PANCAKES

No tricks are needed to get Simon to eat bread—he loves it, almost to the exclusion of everything else on his plate. So I devised several recipes in the bread family that pack an extra nutritional wallop, and now we're both happy.

Puffy Omelette

When making an omelet, try a different technique that makes it puffy and fun: separate the eggs and whip up the egg whites until they are the texture of shaving cream (soft peaks), then mix them with the egg yolks, salt, and pepper and any other flavoring such as grated cheese and/or herbs. Cook in butter or oil in a nonstick pan. You can fold it over or not, as you like.

PUFFY PANCAKES

Makes about fourteen 4-inch pancakes

These are lighter than ordinary pancakes, which makes the extra step of whipping the egg whites worthwhile. We usually eat these pancakes with apple butter, but you can also serve them with maple syrup, to be more traditional.

½ cup all-purpose flour
½ cup whole wheat flour
¼ cup yellow cornmeal
2 tablespoons granulated brown sugar
1½ cups milk
3 eggs, separated

1. Mix the flours, cornmeal, brown sugar, milk, and egg yolks; stir until well blended.

2. Beat the egg whites until stiff and stir into the batter.

3. Drop batter into a lightly greased, hot frying pan and cook on both sides until light brown. Serve when cool enough to eat.

Cooking ahead of time: You can make the first part of the batter (step 1) the night before, and continue with the recipe just before mealtime.

Storage: After I've made all of these pancakes, I freeze the leftovers and use them for snacks or future breakfasts. They defrost in the microwave in just a few seconds.

PEANUT BUTTER BREAD

Makes 1 loaf

My friend Mara Rogers found a recipe similar to this one in an old Hamilton Beach cookbook that looks like it's from the 1940s (there's no copyright page). She adapted it to come up with this recipe, which we both think is delicious. It's a cousin to banana bread, but it isn't too sweet, and it's dense enough to make sandwiches out of, yet moist at the same time. My husband, George, likes to eat slices of this bread toasted for breakfast.

2 cups all-purpose flour
⅔ cup sugar
1 tablespoon baking powder
1½ teaspoons salt
½ teaspoon ground cinnamon
1 cup milk
¾ cup creamy peanut butter
1 egg
4 tablespoons (½ stick) unsalted butter, melted

To Cut Down on Sugar

Keep your sugar in a salt shaker rather than in a bowl, to prevent kids from sprinkling too much on their cereal.

Apple Butter Dip

The first time I fed Simon apple butter, I spread it on a pancake and he wouldn't touch it (a sweet smile followed by, "No thanks . . . I don't like it"). Then I put some apple butter in a tiny dish (an egg cup, actually) and suggested that he might like to dip his plain pancakes into it. He loved it, and has been eating apple butter ever since.

1. Preheat the oven to 350°F.

2. Put all the dry ingredients into the bowl of a food processor and pulse a few times to "sift." Add the remaining ingredients and process just until mixture is blended and smooth.

3. Coat a 9 x 5 x 3-inch baking pan with nonstick baking spray, pour in the batter, and bake for 50 minutes, or until a cake tester inserted in the center comes out clean and the top springs back slightly when touched. Cool before slicing.

Note: You can make this batter in an electric mixer instead of a food processor. Simply follow the instructions as they are written.

Variations: Sometimes, I cut this bread into thin slices to make cream cheese sandwiches, then I soak the sandwich halves in beaten egg and sauté them in butter, to make extra-special French toast!

Wrapped in pretty colored cellophane paper, a loaf of this bread also makes a delicious hostess gift.

Storage: Miraculously, this bread keeps fresh and moist for at least 2 weeks in the refrigerator. If you plan on eating it within a day or two, keep it at room temperature, wrapped airtight.

❄ **X2** 🚶 🛒

SWEET POTATO BISCUITS

Makes about 2 dozen 1½-inch biscuits

Sweet potatoes are so healthful that the Continental Army lived on them for several months during the Revolutionary War. These biscuits taste so good that Simon would happily eat nothing else for just as long.

This is a variation on a Hungarian biscuit called po-gácsa, which I first learned from George's book The Cuisine of Hungary. *The folding is a rudimentary way of leavening the biscuits, since there's no yeast or baking powder. The result is a flaky, many-layered biscuit.*

1 cup whole wheat flour, plus additional flour for rolling out
      dough
1 teaspoon ground cinnamon
½ teaspoon grated nutmeg
½ teaspoon salt
1 cup mashed sweet potatoes (1 medium potato; see Hints)
½ cup (1 stick) unsalted butter, cold and cut into pieces
2 egg yolks

1. Put all the ingredients except one egg yolk into a food processor; process until the dough forms a ball around the blade, or balls up around the edge of the bowl.

2. Remove the dough to a floured board and knead about 10 times. Sprinkle flour underneath and on top of the dough, and roll out to roughly a rectangle—size doesn't matter, but 9 x 15 inches is about right. (Thickness isn't an issue at this point.)

3. Fold the dough in half and refrigerate for 30 minutes (it would be most convenient if you could keep it on the

Lunch Box Tips

■ You can freeze those rectangular juice boxes, and then pack one in a lunch box in the morning to keep the food cool until noontime—by then, the juice will have defrosted and be ready to drink.

■ Here's an idea for a delicious and different kind of lunch box sandwich: cheddar cheese and alfalfa sprouts with mayo on thin white bread.

■ If you'd like to include apple wedges or peach halves in a child's lunch box, dip the cut fruit in orange or grapefruit juice before wrapping in plastic wrap, to keep it from turning brown before lunchtime.

■ To vary the usual lunch box sandwiches, use small biscuits instead of ordinary bread, and pack two or three of these small sandwiches instead of one big one.

same board on which you're rolling it). Take it out of the refrigerator and, keeping the dough folded, roll out again to a 9 x 15-inch rectangle. Fold again and refrigerate for 30 minutes. Repeat this process one more time.

4. Preheat the oven to 350°F. Coat a cookie sheet with nonstick baking spray.

5. Roll out the dough to a ½-inch thickness and cut out rounds of any size you like. Place the biscuits close together on the prepared cookie sheet.

6. Stir together the remaining egg yolk and 1 tablespoon cold water with a fork. Brush the tops of the biscuits with a bit of this egg glaze. Bake for 30 minutes, or until biscuits are golden brown on top and cooked through. Cool before eating. (These biscuits shouldn't be eaten hot, directly from the oven. Their flakiness comes out when they are cooled to room temperature. Later, they can be warmed just slightly before eating, if you wish.)

Hints: You can cook a sweet potato by baking it or boiling it in the skin, like a white potato. When it's cool enough to handle, peel off the skin with a paring knife and put the cooked potato through a ricer or mash it by hand.

Variation: Instead of sweet potato, use mashed winter squash (acorn or butternut squash), fresh or frozen. To make the recipe even easier, use canned mashed pumpkin, which is packed without any sugar or other additives.

If you like your biscuits with a hint of sweetness, add 2 tablespoons of granulated brown sugar to the dough.

Storage: The biscuits will keep for at least 1 week in a tightly closed container in the refrigerator.

❄ **X2** 🏃 🍼

AVOCADO MUFFINS

Makes 5 muffins

This recipe is a good way to use overripe avocados that are too mushy to put into salads. The muffins have a gentle flavor, and are good plain or with a bit of honey on top.

½ cup ripe avocado cubes
1 egg
⅓ cup milk
2 tablespoons orange juice
1 cup whole wheat flour
¼ cup granulated brown sugar
2 teaspoons baking powder
¾ teaspoon ground cinnamon
¼ teaspoon salt

1. Preheat the oven to 350°F. Coat 5 cups of a standard muffin tin with nonstick baking spray.

2. Put the avocado cubes, egg, milk, and orange juice into the bowl of a food processor and process until the mixture is pureed. Add the flour, brown sugar, baking powder, cinnamon, and salt and process until mixed.

3. Spoon an equal amount of the mixture into each of the cups. Tap the muffin tin on the counter a few times to eliminate air bubbles. Bake for 20 minutes, or until the tops of the muffins spring back when touched. Cool on a rack and serve warm or at room temperature.

Storage: These muffins will last for about 1 week in your refrigerator.

Take-Along Milk

Low-fat and regular milk are now available in the same UHT rectangular boxes that juice comes in; you can find them in most big supermarkets. Although they are quite a bit more expensive than refrigerated milk (each box is about 50 cents in my neighborhood), they don't need refrigeration so they are handy to have on short or long trips, or in lunch boxes, and they're less messy than cups.

CORNMEAL CAKES

Makes sixteen 2-inch squares

These savory little squares can be eaten cold, out of hand, as a snack in a stroller, or on a picnic. If you eliminate the cheese, you can serve these warm with syrup or jam for breakfast, as they do in the South.

1 cup yellow cornmeal
1 teaspoon salt
1 cup cold water
3 cups boiling water
½ cup (about 2 ounces) grated Parmesan cheese

1. Coat the inside surfaces of an 8-inch square baking pan with nonstick baking spray.

2. Stir together the cornmeal, salt, and cold water in the top of a double boiler set over simmering water. Gradually pour in boiling water and stir until well blended. Cook, stirring frequently, for 45 minutes. Remove pan from heat and stir in grated cheese.

3. Pour the cornmeal mush into the prepared baking pan and chill in the refrigerator for at least 2 hours.

4. Grease a cutting board with butter or olive oil and turn out the chilled cornmeal square onto the board. Cut into 16 squares, each about 2 inches.

For grown-up kids: To make a more elaborate meal, serve these with a savory tomato sauce.

Storage: These will keep for 5 days in the refrigerator.

✳ **X2** ⫟ 🛒

Coping with Milk Allergy

If a child is allergic to cow's milk, substitute soy infant formula for the milk in almost any simple baking recipe, such as pancakes and muffins.

DUTCH BABY BAKED PANCAKE

Makes 1 pancake

This large, billowy pancake is a specialty of Holland, where student restaurants serve them topped with myriad sweet and savory foods—or just plain, with a dusting of confectioners' sugar and a wedge of lemon. It takes only a few minutes to make, and it's delicious for breakfast, brunch, lunch, or a Sunday night supper.

½ cup all-purpose flour
½ cup milk
2 eggs
2 tablespoons (¼ stick) unsalted butter, melted
Pinch of salt
Confectioners' sugar

1. Preheat the oven to 450°F.

2. While making the batter, put a 7-inch ovenproof skillet into the oven to get hot. Put the flour, milk, eggs, and 1 tablespoon of the melted butter into a food processor or blender and blend until well mixed.

Pancake Project

Simon has always loved to eat bread in every shape and form. When he was younger, I started a Saturday-morning tradition of making whole wheat pancakes. I prepare the batter in the food processor and grind a peeled and cored apple into it. (Nowadays, he cuts up the apple for me.) I make the pancakes the size of a large cookie (about 3 inches in diameter) and Simon eats many of them at a sitting. I freeze the leftover cooked pancakes in packages of two or three, and take them out for breakfast or snacks during the week. To defrost the pancakes, I put them into the toaster oven, and sometimes I spread them with a little peanut butter.

For special occasions, I make a pancake "person" for Simon by pouring a large circle of batter for the body, four small circles of batter for arms and legs (attached to the first circle), and a circle at the top for a head. We use raisins or currants for eyes, and a piece of apple for the mouth.

3. Take the skillet out of the oven and add the remaining tablespoon butter; swirl the pan so the butter coats all surfaces. Quickly pour the batter into the pan and put it into the oven.

4. Bake for 10 minutes, then reduce the oven to 350°F. and bake for 10 minutes more. The sides will puff up beyond the rim of the pan and turn golden brown. Sprinkle with confectioners' sugar and serve when cool enough to eat, cut into wedges.

Variations: Some other toppings for this pancake include syrup, fresh fruit, apple butter, sour cream (or yogurt) and brown sugar, jam, creamed chicken or tuna, cottage cheese, grated cheese, leftover stew, a fried egg, or scrambled eggs.

To make strictly a breakfast or dessert pancake, add the following to the batter: 1 tablespoon grated fresh orange peel or ½ tablespoon dried grated orange peel, a pinch of cinnamon, and a drop of vanilla extract; dust the cooked pancake with confectioners' sugar.

🔲 **X2** 🧍 🛒

CINNAMON-RAISIN FRENCH TOAST

Makes 5 pieces of toast

John Doherty is the executive chef of the Waldorf-Astoria Hotel in New York City, where he is responsible for serving up to 7,000 quality meals every day. John's wife, Donna, feeds their two children—Jennarose, five, and Patrick, three—which is perhaps an equally perplexing job. This is one of the recipes she relies on.

2 eggs
1½ tablespoons milk
2 teaspoons orange juice
1 teaspoon maple syrup
⅛ teaspoon vanilla extract
⅛ teaspoon ground cinnamon
Pinch of salt
1 tablespoon unsalted butter
5 slices Pepperidge Farm Cinnamon Raisin Bread
Maple syrup

Cottage Cheese and Yogurt with Diced Fruit

You can start with cottage cheese already mixed with pineapple, or plain cottage cheese—in either case, try to buy cottage cheese that is 4 percent minimum milkfat, so your child is getting as many calories as possible (unless, of course, your child has a weight problem or your family has a history of high cholesterol). Then add an equal amount of plain yogurt and stir in diced apples, pears, bananas, or berries.

Granola–Cottage Cheese Breakfast

One of Simon's favorite breakfasts is cottage cheese mixed with granola. I don't usually have time to make my own granola, so I buy a good brand that's made without refined sugar, but has lots of dried fruit and nuts in it. Sometimes we stir in some plain yogurt, too.

1. Combine the eggs, milk, juice, syrup, vanilla, cinnamon, and salt by beating with a fork or wire whisk in a shallow bowl.

2. Melt the butter in a large nonstick skillet over medium heat.

3. Soak the bread slices in the egg mixture for about 20 seconds on each side, and place in skillet, cooking on each side until light brown. Serve with just a drizzle of maple syrup.

Storage: Leftovers can be kept in the refrigerator for 2 days, and reheated in the microwave.

🔲 ❄ **X2** 🚶

Breads, Muffins, and Pancakes

DAVID BURKE'S PEANUT BUTTER FRENCH TOAST

Makes 1 sandwich

David Burke, executive chef of the lovely River Café in Brooklyn, New York, finds that the following dish is one often requested by his two boys, Connor and Dillon. He serves the sandwiches plain or with maple syrup.

2 slices white or whole wheat bread
2 tablespoons creamy peanut butter
1 tablespoon minced banana (optional)
1 egg plus 2 tablespoons milk, blended together
1½ tablespoons unsalted butter
Maple syrup (optional)

1. Make a peanut butter sandwich using the bread, peanut butter, and banana. Cut into 4 squares.

2. Put the sandwich squares into the egg and milk mixture and turn to soak both sides.

3. In the meantime, melt the butter in a medium skillet over medium heat. Put the soaked sandwich squares into the butter in the pan, lower heat, and cook both sides until golden brown and the peanut butter on the inside of the sandwiches is warm and soft.

Storage: Leftovers can be kept in the refrigerator for 2 days.

Toast Pictures

For a fun food project, make toast pictures. Put a small amount of milk in a cup and add a few drops of food coloring. You and the child each take a slice of spongy white bread (like Wonder Bread) and, using a clean brush, paint them with the colored milk. Toast the bread, then the painting will show up clearly. Then, of course, you can eat your work.

Another way to make toast pictures is to buy cookie cutters in animal shapes and press them into bread about three-fourths of the way through the slice. Toast the slices, and the animal shapes will show up on the toast.

SNACKS AND SWEETS

I'm not so radical that I want to keep Simon away completely from all sweets, but I *do* want him to appreciate those that are wholesome and good tasting. The following recipes definitely count as dessert, but they've got nutritional benefits as well.

Snacks are yet another problem, and I've included a few suggestions that I've found helpful.

RAISIN BREAD PUDDING

Makes about 6 cups

Upperclass English men and women often fondly remember the bread pudding made by their nannies. It was probably first invented by some practical housewife who didn't want to throw away stale bread. It's so good, however, that today's cooks usually make it from fresh bread. It's also good for you, full of protein from the eggs and milk, and iron and other nutrients from the fruit.

3 cups raisin-bread cubes, crusts removed, spread out on a
  cookie sheet and left overnight to get stale (see Hints)
½ cup diced dried fruit
2 tablespoons (¼ stick) unsalted butter, cold and cut into
  small pieces
3 eggs
3 egg yolks
2 cups milk
¾ cup granulated brown or white sugar
1 teaspoon vanilla extract

1. Preheat the oven to 350°F. Coat a 6- or 8-cup oven-proof dish with nonstick baking spray.

2. Put bread cubes, diced fruit, and butter pieces into the baking pan and stir lightly to mix. In a separate bowl, whisk together the eggs, egg yolks, milk, sugar, and vanilla. Pour over the bread mixture and let stand at room temperature for 30 minutes.

Make Your Own Raisins

Here's a fun project you can do with your child: make your own raisins. Buy some ripe, firm seedless Thompson green grapes and wash and dry them thoroughly. Remove the grapes from their stems and spread in one layer on a paper plate or plastic tray. Cover the tray with cheesecloth and fasten the cloth so it will not blow off. Place the tray outside in direct sunlight where the air can circulate around the grapes. Bring the tray inside every evening, and place it back in the sunshine in the morning. After four days, test the raisins and see if they are dry enough; if not, put the tray back in the sun for another day or so.

3. Bake for 40 to 50 minutes, or until a knife inserted into the center of the pudding comes out clean. Serve when cool enough to eat.

Hints: You can use any kind of raisin bread for this recipe. Usually, I buy unsliced whole wheat raisin-honey bread in the health food store and cut it into ½-inch cubes.

To dry the bread in a hurry, put the cubes on a cookie sheet in a 350°F. oven for 5 minutes. Of course, if you already have *stale* raisin bread on hand, you're one step ahead in this recipe.

Variations: Mixed dried fruit, already diced, is sold in the supermarket in cellophane packages marked "fruit bits." You can also use raisins or currants, or dice any other kind of single dried fruit, such as apples or apricots.

Use cream or half-and-half in place of the milk in this recipe, if calories and cholesterol are not a problem for you or your child. I sometimes use light or heavy cream, just to give Simon some *extra* calories.

Storage: This will keep in your refrigerator for up to 5 days. It can be served cold or warm.

X2

BROWN RICE PUDDING

Makes 2 cups

This is rice pudding made the old-fashioned way. It only takes a few minutes to assemble the ingredients, but the cooking takes a while. You can make it when you're in the kitchen working on something else, since it needs little tending. The results are worth it.

I first learned a version of this recipe when I worked in the pastry department of the old "21" Club restaurant. It's the ultimate nursery dessert, soothing and full of good nutrition, perfect for a sick child—or a well one, for that matter, not to mention his parents!

2 tablespoons sugar
3 cups milk
1 cup heavy cream
Pinch of salt
1 vanilla bean (see Hint)
6 tablespoons brown rice

An Ounce of Prevention

Any food that is high in sugar will cause a child's teeth to decay—especially if the food is sticky to boot—and that includes raisins and other dried fruits. The best way to counteract this effect is to get your child into the habit of drinking a glass of water after eating raisins or any other food containing a lot of sugar.

Storage Hint

All whole grains and whole-grain products, such as whole wheat flour, brown rice, or rye flour, should be kept in airtight containers in the refrigerator, because of their tendency to go rancid more quickly than refined products.

1. Put the sugar, milk, cream, salt, and vanilla bean in a small, heavy pot and bring to a boil. Lower the heat and add the rice, stirring. Adjust the heat so the mixture bubbles slowly.

2. Cover the pot and cook, stirring occasionally, for 1 hour and 15 minutes. Turn off the heat, keep the cover on the pot, and allow to rest for 10 minutes. Remove the vanilla bean and discard. Serve warm, or refrigerate and serve chilled.

Hint: Use only one vanilla bean, no matter how much you are making.

Variations: If you like raisins in your rice pudding, stir them in (about ¼ cup) just as the pudding comes off the heat.

To serve this the way they do at the "21" Club, spoon the cooked pudding into individual heatproof serving dishes and spread a ½-inch layer of whipped cream over the top of each one. Just before serving, place the dish under the broiler until the topping is light brown.

To reduce the fat and cholesterol contents: Substitute additional milk for the heavy cream.

Storage: You can keep this cooked pudding in the refrigerator for up to 4 days.

X2 🚶 🛒

DANIEL BOULUD'S SWEET APPLE ALIX

Makes 2 cups

Daniel Boulud is the chef of the justly famed Le Cirque restaurant in New York City. His little girl Alix is two years old, and her father has been making this dish for her since she was tiny. I think it also makes a great dessert for an adult dinner party.

5 McIntosh apples, peeled and cored
1 lemon
½ vanilla bean, split in half lengthwise
1 sprig fresh mint *or* ½ teaspoon dried mint
3 tablespoons granulated sugar
¼ cup water
½ cup heavy cream
1 tablespoon confectioners' sugar
2 tablespoons grated sweetened chocolate (see Hint)

1. Cut the apples into ½-inch chunks. Grate the peel of the lemon, then squeeze the juice. In a small saucepan, put the apple chunks, grated lemon peel, lemon juice, split vanilla bean, mint sprig or dried mint, granulated sugar, and the water. Cover the pan and cook over medium-low heat until the apple is very soft, 20 to 30 minutes, stirring frequently. Discard the vanilla bean and mint sprig (unless you've used dried mint).

Neatness Counts

A pizza cutter makes a handy tool for cutting neat squares of a rectangular cake or a tray of fudge.

2. Pour the cooked apple into a small shallow serving dish and spread evenly. Let cool in the refrigerator.

3. Whip the cream with the confectioners' sugar until it reaches the consistency of shaving cream (soft peaks). Spread the cream evenly over the apples in the dish.

4. To serve, sprinkle the chocolate over the whipped cream and serve with cookies.

Hint: Use milk chocolate or dark chocolate, depending on which kind you like. An ordinary candy bar (without nuts) works well; grate it in a food processor fitted with the metal blade.

Variation: If you are in a hurry, put the dish together using storebought applesauce in a jar, readymade whipped cream, and chocolate sprinkles.

Cooking ahead of time: You can cook the apples and refrigerate them (through step 2) up to 24 hours ahead of time. If the chocolate is already grated, all you need to do before serving is whip the cream and put the dish together (steps 3 and 4).

ORANGE PINEAPPLE CAKE

Makes one 9-inch cake

I found a version of this cake recipe (really more of a coffeecake) at the Pillsbury Bake-Off in Phoenix in February 1990. It was submitted by Nancy Labrie from Rye, New Hampshire; she suggests garnishing it with orange slices and mint leaves. I like it because it not only tastes good but also contains very little sugar—the pineapple and orange juice sweeten it nicely.

1 (8-ounce) can crushed pineapple, packed without sugar

1½ cups self-rising flour *or* 1½ cups all-purpose flour,
2 teaspoons baking powder, and ¾ teaspoon salt

1 cup whole wheat flour

⅓ cup granulated brown sugar

½ cup orange juice

⅓ cup unsalted butter, melted

½ to 1 teaspoon grated orange rind

1 egg, lightly beaten

½ cup confectioners' sugar

1. Preheat the oven to 400°F. Grease the bottom of a 9-inch round cake pan. Drain the pineapple, reserving the juice.

2. In a large bowl, combine the flours and brown sugar. In another bowl, combine the drained pineapple, orange juice, melted butter, orange rind, and egg; blend well, then add to dry ingredients all at once. By hand, stir until dry ingredients are just moistened.

3. Spread dough in greased pan. Bake for about 25 minutes, or until light golden brown and a toothpick inserted in the center comes out clean. Cool 1 minute, then remove from pan to a serving tray or stand.

4. Put the confectioners' sugar in a small bowl and moisten with enough of the reserved pineapple juice for desired drizzling consistency. Drizzle over warm cake. Serve warm or at room temperature.

Storage: This cake will last, covered in an airtight container, for 2 days at room temperature.

❄ **X2** 🚶 👶

PEANUT BUTTER AND JELLY BIRTHDAY CAKE WITH MILK CHOCOLATE FROSTING

Makes 1 sheet cake, 9 x 13 inches, which cuts into twelve 3-inch squares

I made this for Simon's second birthday party, and it was a big hit with the kids and *the grownups—the children devoured their cake, and everyone had seconds. It tastes like a cross between a peanut butter and jelly sandwich and a giant Reese's Peanut Butter Cup. I plan to make it a tradition by preparing it for Simon's birthday every year.*

1 cup creamy peanut butter
⅔ cup lightly salted butter, at room temperature
2 cups granulated brown sugar
6 eggs
2 teaspoons vanilla extract
2 cups all-purpose flour
2 teaspoons baking powder
½ teaspoon salt
¾ cup milk
1 (10-ounce) jar no-sugar-added grape jelly (optional)
1 recipe Milk Chocolate Frosting *or* Easiest Chocolate
     Frosting (recipes follow)

1. Preheat the oven to 350°F. Grease and flour a 9 x 13 x 2-inch sheet pan.

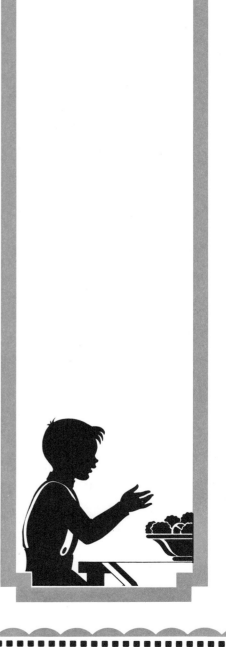

For a Neat Birthday Cake

Small marshmallows or Life Savers make good holders for candles on a birthday cake; they prevent the wax from dripping onto the frosting.

2. Put the peanut butter and butter into a food processor and process until blended. Add the brown sugar, process again until mixed, and scrape the sides of the bowl. Add the eggs, 1 at a time, pulsing the processor after each egg is added. Add the vanilla.

3. In a bowl, mix the dry ingredients and add half of the dry mixture to the processor. Process for a few seconds, then add half the milk and process again. Repeat these steps.

4. Transfer the batter to the prepared pan. Bake for 40 minutes, or until a toothpick inserted in the center comes out clean and the top springs back when touched. Cool by placing the sheet pan on a wire rack.

5. When completely cool, carefully remove the cake from the pan and place it on the serving platter. You can do this by turning the platter upside down and placing it on the top of the pan; turn the platter and pan over at the same time and tap the bottom of the pan to loosen the cake. The cake should then drop onto the platter and you can remove the pan.

6. If you decide to fill the cake with jelly, cut it in half horizontally and turn the top half onto a piece of wax paper or foil. Spread the jelly on the bottom half of the cake, and replace the top. Then proceed to frost the cake.

Storage: You can make and fill this cake ahead of time, wrap it airtight, and freeze it for up to a month. Thaw it—still in its freezer packing—in the refrigerator for 24 hours before frosting.

MILK CHOCOLATE FROSTING

Makes 3 cups

2 sticks (½ pound) unsalted butter, chilled
⅔ cup unsweetened cocoa powder
3½ cups confectioners' sugar
½ cup milk
1 teaspoon vanilla extract

1. Cream the butter in an electric mixer. Add the cocoa and beat for about 2 minutes, or until well blended, scraping the sides of the bowl occasionally.

2. Alternately add the confectioners' sugar and the milk, beating about 3 minutes, or until very smooth. Beat in the vanilla.

3. Refrigerate frosting until ready to use. If it's too cold to spread on top of the cake, put the frosting back into the mixer and beat it until it's supple again.

Storage: The frosting will keep for 2 days in the refrigerator.

Easiest Chocolate Frosting

If you decide not to fill your cake with jelly, you can make a super-simple frosting in this way. Sprinkle a small (6-ounce) package of chocolate chips (either semisweet or milk chocolate) over the cake just as it comes out of the oven and is still in its baking pan. Let stand for about 5 minutes, until the chips become shiny and soft. At that point they will be completely melted and you can spread them over the top of the cake with a knife or a spatula, for an instant frosting.

Super Special Ice Cream Cone Tips

- Place a marshmallow in the bottom of an ice cream cone to prevent leakage.

- For a fun party treat, prepare a boxed cake mix batter and half-fill flat-bottomed ice cream cones with it; bake at 350°F. for 20 minutes and, when cool, add a scoop of ice cream.

JASPER WHITE'S TAPIOCA-APPLE PUDDING, FOR J.P.

Makes 1½ cups

Jasper White, owner of the celebrated Jasper's restaurant in Boston, created this dish for his eighteen-month-old son, Jasper Paul.

2 tablespoons pearl tapioca (see Hint)
1 cup milk
1 egg yolk
½ cup applesauce (with no added sugar)

1. In a small, heavy saucepan, combine the tapioca and milk. Cover with plastic wrap and refrigerate for 2 hours.

2. Remove the tapioca from the refrigerator, and place the pot over medium heat and bring to a low boil. Reduce the heat and simmer for 10 minutes, stirring frequently, until the tapioca is translucent but still firm.

3. Mix the egg yolk and applesauce together and whip into the warm tapioca until well blended. Simmer and stir for 2 more minutes. Pour the pudding into a serving bowl or individual dishes and chill.

Hint: Pearl tapioca has a better texture than quick-cooking tapioca. If you use the quick-cooking type, follow the directions on the box but omit the sugar and add ½ cup fruit puree for each cup of pudding.

Variations: Use this recipe as a master and substitute pear, banana, apricot, or any other cooked fruit purees.

X2

PEAR SORBET SUNDAE

Makes about 2 cups

This is a lovely "special occasion" way to eat fruit. It's another one of Helen Chardack's ingenious recipes.

1 cup plus 1 tablespoon pear juice
1 teaspoon lemon juice
1 medium pear
1 tablespoon raisins
1½ teaspoons granulated brown sugar
½ tablespoon unsalted butter
¼ teaspoon almond extract
2 tablespoons vanilla yogurt

1. Pour 1 cup of the pear juice and the lemon juice into a shallow dish or tray, such as an ice cube tray without the dividers, and place in the freezer until solid, at least 3 hours.

Stir-Fried Fruit

David Burke, executive chef of the romantic River Café in Brooklyn, had an inspiration for feeding children in a dish he calls Stir-Fried Fruit, which he serves over ice cream or sorbet, or with whipped cream; it also tastes great on its own or over pound cake.

David cuts ripe fruit into bite-size pieces,

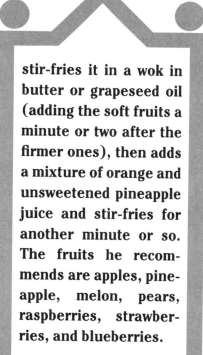

stir-fries it in a wok in butter or grapeseed oil (adding the soft fruits a minute or two after the firmer ones), then adds a mixture of orange and unsweetened pineapple juice and stir-fries for another minute or so. The fruits he recommends are apples, pineapple, melon, pears, raspberries, strawberries, and blueberries.

2. Peel, core, and dice the pear. Place in a small saucepan with the raisins, 1 tablespoon pear juice, brown sugar, butter, and almond extract. Cover and cook over medium heat, stirring occasionally, until apples are tender, about 15 minutes. Let the pears cool in this liquid. (You can also do this step in the microwave.)

3. Scrape the block of frozen pear juice with a fork and put these ice crystals into a serving dish. Spoon the cooked pear compote over the ice crystals, top with yogurt, and serve.

Variations: An apple and apple juice combination works just as well in this recipe, but use vanilla extract instead of almond.

Cooking ahead of time: You can make the compote and freeze the pear juice up to 2 days ahead of time. When it's time to serve, begin with step 3.

❄ **X2** 🚶 👶

PHYLLIS RICHMAN'S OATMEAL COOKIES

Makes about 18 cookies

Phyllis Richman is the food editor of the Washington Post, *and has successfully raised three healthy children. The following is one of her tried-and-true recipes. She points out that, "while the cookies take patience, they are very good and among the few cookie recipes that use no wheat flour."*

½ cup (1 stick) unsalted butter

1 cup sugar

4 eggs, separated

2 cups quick-cooking rolled oats

Pinch of salt

1 teaspoon baking powder

Coping with After-Nap Crankiness

Is your child excessively cranky when he gets up from his nap? Simon often is, and the crankiness usually abates as soon as I give him something to eat or to drink that contains sugar—a box of juice or a fruit-juice–sweetened cookie.

1. Preheat the oven to 350°F.

2. Cream the butter and sugar. Add the egg yolks, oats, salt, and baking powder.

3. Beat the egg whites until stiff and fold into the butter-sugar mixture (see Note).

4. Drop mixture by Ping-Pong ball–sized gobs onto a lightly greased cookie sheet (a paper liner for the cookie sheet would make the job of removing the cookies easier). Bake for 8 to 12 minutes, or until lightly browned.

Note: Phyllis adds, "This dough is quite stiff for folding in egg whites; just do it as lightly as possible."

Storage: These cookies will keep for 5 days in an airtight container.

PHYLLIS BOLOGNA'S GINGERBREAD FAMILY

Phyllis Bologna is the executive chef of General Foods and the mother of eight-year-old Carey. When she sent me this recipe, she also included these comments: "I started making this recipe for my son Carey's first Christmas. As he got older he would help pat out or roll the dough. Eventually we have graduated to gingerbread houses. The most important part has been that we make gingerbread dads, moms, and kids, not just gingerbread boys. It has now become a tradition for me to teach our friends' children how to make the gingerbread family when they are about four years old. After what is always an eventful day in the kitchen, they are rewarded with their own set of cookie cutters—and of course they get to take their cookies home."

1½ cups molasses

1½ cups (3 sticks) unsalted butter *or* margarine

7⅓ cups all-purpose flour

1½ cups granulated brown sugar

4 teaspoons ground ginger

4 teaspoons ground cinnamon

2 teaspoons baking powder

1 teaspoon salt

2 eggs

Homemade Play Dough

Simon's first teacher, Gail Ionesco of the Poppyseed Pre-Nursery in New York City, gave me this recipe for the terrific homemade play dough her pupils use all year long: 2 cups all-purpose flour, 2 cups water, 1 cup salt, 1 tablespoon cream of tartar, ¼ cup oil, a few drops of food coloring; cook this mixture over medium heat for 3 minutes, stirring constantly, until it reaches the consistency of mashed potatoes; let it cool, then knead and store in an airtight container.

1. In a medium saucepan (with a nonstick surface, if you have one), heat the molasses over low heat until it is simmering. Add the butter or margarine and stir to dissolve. Remove from heat and let cool for 15 minutes.

2. Sift together the flour, brown sugar, ginger, cinnamon, baking powder, and salt. Stir in the molasses mixture and mix well. Stir in the eggs. Divide the dough into 4 parts and wrap each with plastic wrap or wax paper; refrigerate for 1 to 2 hours.

3. After the dough has chilled, preheat the oven to 375°F. Coat several cookie sheets with nonstick baking spray.

4. Working with 1 piece of the dough at a time, roll or pat out the dough on a floured board until it is approximately ¼ inch thick. Cut into desired shapes with cookie cutters. Decorate with raisins, nuts, chocolate chips, or dried fruit. Bake for 15 to 20 minutes, until the edges of the cookies are just beginning to brown. Remove cookies from sheets and cool on wire racks.

Note: If you want to hang your cookies on the tree, cut 1-inch lengths of paper drinking straws and push through the dough at the top of the cookies before baking. Remove the straws while cookies are still warm. Put string, ribbon, or yarn through the holes to hang cookies.

Storage: Cookies will last 1 week refrigerated in an airtight container.

❄ **X2** 🚶 🛒

NEW SNACK IDEAS

■ A ball of peanut butter rolled in toasted sesame seeds.

■ Pitted prunes stuffed with peanut butter or ricotta cheese.

■ Even though we eat it for fun, popcorn qualifies as a healthful grain product, and is a great addition to a child's diet (especially if it's made in a forced-air popper).

■ Animal crackers made with whole wheat flour and without refined sugar are sold in health food stores. These come in cute boxes with handles. (Okay, so the boxes are not quite as cute as the ones you knew as a child, with string handles and all, but the cookies inside are much better for you.)

■ A commercial version of the Rice Krispies squares we used to make from the recipe on the back of the box is available today in health food stores. Made with brown rice instead, they're crunchy and make good snacks, especially since they are individually wrapped—a definite plus with kids.

■ Brown rice crackers, the puffy ones called "cakes," come large and small, and some are flavored. They're satisfyingly crispy, but I tend to buy only the plain ones, since the flavored ones are sticky (especially those made with fruit juice).

■ Carrot puffs, like cheese curls, are made only with carrots and are not fried; they are crunchy and absolutely addictive. Simon and I race each other to see who can get to the bottom of the bag first.

■ Cranberry juice with no sugar (or anything else) added is sold in health food stores. It's one of the best sources of vitamin C you can find, and was first recommended to me by Simon's doctor. But it's naturally sour, so it needs to be cut by about one-third with another pure—sweet—fruit juice such as apple, pear, or grape juice. Cranberry juice cocktail that you buy in the supermarket is mixed with sugar and other ingredients to sweeten it.

■ Fig bars, sold in health food stores, are a healthful alternative to Fig Newtons. Made with whole wheat flour, various kinds of dried fruits, and no refined sugar, these have been a staple in our pantry since Simon was small. When Simon gets up at 5:00 A.M.—all too often for my liking—I can give him one of these and a box of juice and he's set until our family breakfast, at about 8:00 A.M. We even leave one of these for Santa Claus every year, by the fireplace with a glass of milk.

■ Fruit roll-ups made only with fruit, and without additives or sugar, are a favorite with kids.

■ Anything that is dried is highly concentrated, and that includes all the harmful pesticides that are used in cultivation. Therefore, organic dried fruit—and that means raisins, too—is a much safer bet than dried fruit grown conventionally.

■ Sweet potato chips are full of nutrients, and full of the crunch that kids love. They are sold in bags the way ordinary potato chips are.

■ Seven-grain and whole wheat waffles, sold frozen, are quickly prepared by popping them into a toaster oven for a few minutes. We top them with various things: fruit and cottage cheese, apple butter, peanut butter and—for a treat—ice cream.

HAPPY BIRTHDAY

After only four years, we've established a tradition for Simon's birthday. He was born in August, so he can have an outdoor party, with lots of kids (by choice, I have broken the rule about having only one more guest than the age of the child), and that means lots of parents, too. We go to our country house, about an hour north of New York City, which offers many outdoor activities: swimming in a kiddie pool, swingset play, rowboat rides on the lake—and pony rides on Ginger, a four-legged guest.

We send invitations in the form of balloons. First we blow up sturdy balloons, then we write the pertinent information on them with permanent felt markers. After the ink dries, we deflate the balloons, and send them to our friends, who have to blow them up again to read them.

For the party, I borrow all the kid-size chairs I need and set them up on our deck at small tables, in an effort to organize the meal service as much as possible. Each child's place is marked with a balloon tied to his chair with his name on it. (After the party, we are careful to dispose of the balloons at home, because of possible danger to sea animals from balloons that float out over the ocean.) I also mark each child's paper cup with his or her name, so that they don't get mixed up during the festivities.

The luncheon menu gets lots of attention, as you might imagine. I've found that a buffet with options is a hit with everyone. Our most successful menu came almost entirely from this book:

APPETIZERS

Quesadillas (page 140)

Baby Egg Rolls (page 125)

Baby Ganouj (page 142)
with a selection of raw vegetables for dipping

LUNCH

Turkey and Veggie Chili (page 90)
accompanied by brown rice, white rice, grated cheese,
minced jalapeño peppers, diced tomatoes, and minced scallions

Avocado Muffins (page 156)

Cornmeal Cakes (page 157)

DESSERT

Peanut Butter and Jelly Birthday Cake
with Milk Chocolate Frosting (page 172)
(every year in a different shape—
last year it was Dumbo, this year it's a dinosaur)

Ice Cream in Individual Cups

CODA

When Simon was an infant, and it was time to start feeding him solid food, I worried that I'd make a mistake. I wanted my child to eat good food that was nutritious, but I didn't want to be fanatical about his diet. I wanted him to eat a variety of things, so neither he nor I would get bored. (No "If it's Tuesday, then it must be meatloaf night" for this household!) Mostly I just wanted to relax about that aspect of raising my little boy. I have accomplished these things for me and Simon, and I hope our book has had the same effect on you and the little ones you love.

THANKS

Because George and I have been in the business of creating good food—together and separately—for so many years, we have had a chance to get to know some very talented cooks. When Simon was born, I decided to ask them how they feed their own kids. Many have found the same thing I have: the task of nourishing your own children day in and day out can be somewhat more daunting than turning out three hundred impeccable meals daily in an acclaimed restaurant.

Several of the recipes and ideas in this book were generously given to me by these creative people. Simon and I have tested all of the

Thanks

recipes provided by the chefs and their spouses, and found them to be delicious; we both say thanks.

I would also like to thank two more gifted cooks, Mara Reid Rogers and Hillary Davis, who helped out with the testing of the recipes herein.

My editor, Peter Guzzardi, provided all kinds of invaluable support, not the least of which was a modern American father's point of view. Harriet Bell, before she left the fold, gave both editorial advice and mother-to-mother guidance, and I am grateful for both. And, of course, I hope I never have to write a book without Pam Thomas's assistance—I don't care how lofty her advancement.

Special thanks to Lisa Ekus, who became a mother before I did, and is a wonderful role model.

I am also thankful to George, for our blessed life together, and for giving me Simon, who is the fruit of our love for each other. The three of us can live on that desert island happily ever after.

INDEX

Index

Index

Index